Mollys Folly
Marston
Foston
Lodge
Foston
Three Shire Bush
Bennington Field F.
Hindwell
Lodge
Thorkson Well
Nova Scotia
Great North Road
Sewstern Lane
W. Allington
E. Allington
Gonerby Moor F.
Saltwell
Belton
Nottingham
and Grantham Railway
Station
Wheatsheaf
Muston
Sedgebrook
Barrowby Thorns
Great Go
Willow Bridge
Muston Mill
Barrowby Vale
Barrowby Parsonage F.
Millhill
Muston Bridge
Breederhill
Longore Bridge
Lock
Old Beck
Old Hall
Casthorpe Hills
Barrowby
Muston Gorse Bridge
River Devon
Muston Gorse Fox Cover
Casthorpe
Belvoir Lane
Barrowby Lodge
Woolsthorpe Wharf
Lock
Woolsthorpe Lodge
Earlsfields
Harlaxton Cavs
Barrowby Mires
Woolsthorpe
Denton Lodge
Reservoir
Wharf
Ruins of Woolsthorpe Old Church
Harlaxton Inn
Denton
Harlaxton

The Book of Bottesford 1989
has been published
in a Limited Edition
of which this is

Number   447   *John M. Simpson*

A list of subscribers
has been printed
at the back of the book

Michael Honeybone.

THE BOOK OF BOTTESFORD

Fleming Bridge, Bottesford. (VPE)

The spire and railway crossing leading to Beacon Hill. (VPE)

THE BOOK OF BOTTESFORD

CONTINUITY AND CHANGE
IN A LEICESTERSHIRE VILLAGE

BY

MICHAEL HONEYBONE

BARRACUDA BOOKS LIMITED
BUCKINGHAM, ENGLAND
MCMLXXXIX

PUBLISHED BY BARRACUDA BOOKS LIMITED
BUCKINGHAM, ENGLAND
AND PRINTED BY
THOMSON LITHO LIMITED
GLASGOW, SCOTLAND

BOUND BY
CHARLES LETTS LIMITED
DALKEITH, SCOTLAND

JACKETS PRINTED BY
CHENEY & SONS LIMITED
BANBURY, OXON

LITHOGRAPHY BY
SOUTH MIDLANDS LITHOPLATES LIMITED
LUTON, ENGLAND

TYPESET BY
HARPER PHOTOTYPESETTERS LIMITED
NORTHAMPTON, ENGLAND

© Michael Honeybone 1989

ISBN 0 86023 411 8

Contents

ENDPAPERS — FRONT: Bottesford country, from the First Edition,
Ordnance Survey; BACK: part of the Parish, from the early 20th
century Ordnance Survey map.

Acknowledgements

This history of a parish is created by the local people. It has been a great pleasure to write this account of Bottesford, some of it directly from the words of the villagers themselves. In particular I have been given several accounts of life in Bottesford prepared by people who lived here at the end of the nineteenth and the beginning of the twentieth centuries. These first-hand descriptions of village life are printed as appendices. I thank the present day representatives of the writers: Mrs Dorothy Beedham, Mr Philip Sutton and Mr Arnold Jordan.

These accounts of village life have formed the basis of some enjoyable meetings of the Bottesford Local History Society. The Society has been the inspiration of this book. Since 1971, well-informed and thoughtful members have listened politely to my views, have tolerated my prejudices, but most of all they have discussed the nature of the parish in which they live. If this book brings Bottesford's past to life, it is a result of the great enthusiasm of members of that Society.

I have been able to call upon the services of three experts in their field. Mr Vaughan Evans has both painted lovely pictures and drawn informative maps. Mr Ted Rayson has taken excellent photographs of Bottesford over the years and has produced many more specially for this book. Mrs Sheila Harris has typed the drafts of the book with enthusiasm. I am grateful to them all for their hard work.

The staff of the Leicestershire Library Service at Melton and Bottesford have kindly held subscription lists and coped thoughtfully with my many enquiries. The archaeological services at county level in Leicestershire have now been computerised and the read-out on Bottesford proved invaluable. The county archaeologists were encouraging and answered many queries. As always, the staff of the Leicestershire Record Office proved both helpful and knowledgeable.

The pleasure involved in writing this book has been enhanced by the many friendships resulting from it. It has been both exciting and rewarding to contact families associated with Bottesford in wartime. I have learnt a considerable amount from *For the Duration*, the book written by Flt Sgt Hawes' niece, Mrs Denise Rope. Finally, I would like to thank Diana and Alison Honeybone who have worked hard towards the production of this book.

Dedication

For the people of Bottesford and Muston

Foreword

by Alan Reed, Headmaster and Warden,
Belvoir High School and Bottesford Community Centre

In 1831, Samuel Taylor Coleridge wrote 'If men could learn from history, what lessons it might teach us'.

If Michael Honeybone's biggest challenge when writing *The Vale of Belvoir* was to define its area, writing a book about Bottesford must have been equally difficult – not that there is a dearth of information about the village; quite the contrary. The challenge on this occasion has been to identify the individuality of a Leicestershire village with a Nottingham postal address yet closely affiliated to its nearest market town, Grantham in Lincolnshire.

There are many lessons to be learnt from this book, the first of which is that the villagers of Bottesford have always exploited its geographical position to great advantage. It has been a staging post throughout the centuries. It has, therefore, never suffered from rural isolation and has been able to meet the depredations of plagues, famine and occasional floods with remarkable resilience and fortitude. Above all it has been a caring community, supporting those in need as only a village can.

Throughout this book, powerful personalities emerge from its pages, making their mark on the village at a particular point in its history. Their names have lived on.

The true character of a village can be identified only if one has lived in it or been associated with it for some considerable time. However, with this book as a guide, your knowledge of the village will be deepened and you will begin to understand the pride and determination of its residents to protect their heritage.

Alan Reed,

Preface

by Kenneth A. Dyke, Rector of Bottesford

Beautiful Bottesford – that it certainly is to resident and visitor alike from all over the world.

One of the great joys of this work is how families started in earliest times and have continued to this present day – from the early Lords of Belvoir to tradesmen and women whose half a dozen or so names are still very much to the fore.

The social, political and economic story of the area is very clear, from earliest times to the present day.

In early history feudal lords were not noted for their care or concern for others. This is not the case here, however but quite the reverse.

Kenneth A. Dyke

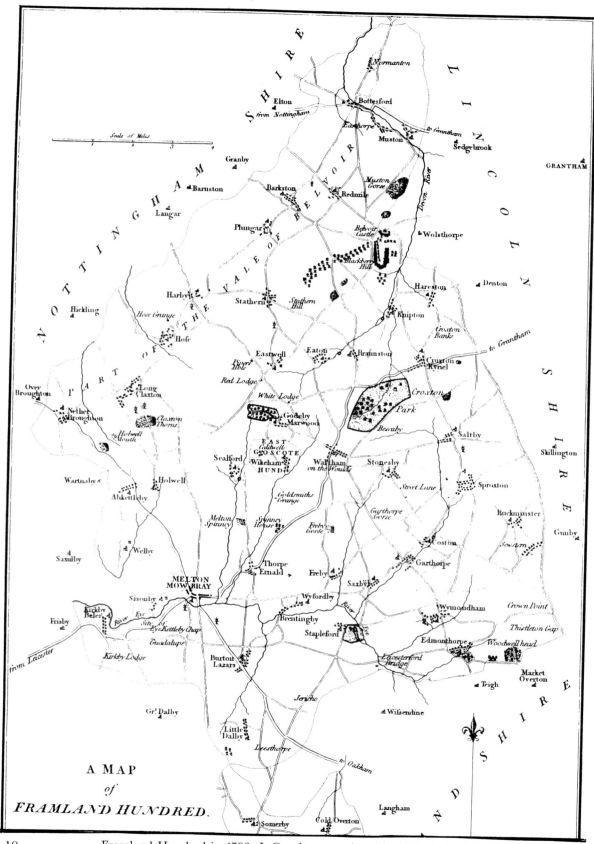

A MAP

of

FRAMLAND HUNDRED.

Framland Hundred in 1792. J. Cary's map printed in Nichols. (JN)

Introduction

Bottesford is one of the largest parishes in Leicestershire. Its 5,000 acres stretch for five miles, from the most north-easterly point of the county at Three Shire Bush, to the northern edge of the Belvoir Castle hills. To the west is Nottinghamshire; to the east Lincolnshire and the neighbouring parish of Muston, which was joined to Bottesford civil parish in 1936 and to the ecclesiastical parish in 1961. The hamlet of Normanton is separated from the village of Bottesford by the gentle rise of Beacon Hill, today called Palmer's Hill by local people. The village consists of several distinct parts, each with its own name. The area to the east of the Cross has always been known as Easthorpe. To the north of the church the old name of Beckingthorpe is still retained by an extensive farmhouse, which used to be part of the Rutland Estate. The name of Wimbishthorpe has recently been revived in a street name in the north-west of the village. Centuries ago, Easthorpe to the east was balanced by Westhorpe to the west, but this name has disappeared today in favour of the West End.

Throughout recorded history the whole parish has been extensively farmed. Cornland and grazing land have predominated alternatively, according to local or national demands. A complex open-field system developed, based on three huge fields serving Normanton, Easthorpe and Bottesford. The pattern of farming was continuously changed, especially to sheep pasture after the Black Death, and to water meadows in the eighteenth century. Recently grain has predominated, after a century or so of heavy grazing and dairying. As twentieth century mechanisation developed, so the heavy clay soils no longer demanded the drudgery of innumerable labourers. In the 1940s a new land use brought hundreds of newcomers to this old-established rural community: many acres were covered by the concrete and huts of an aerodrome and petrol supply camp in the Second World War.

But this change was only one of a whole range of similar interruptions to the pattern of farming life. Ten French soldiers of fortune settled here in 1066; there was a major civil war garrison employed in 1644 and 1645 to reduce Belvoir Castle. The turnpike roads, the canal and most especially the railway, bringing extensive employment, ended rural isolation. It would indeed be quite wrong to think of the parish as ever having been an idyllic and isolated rural environment. On the contrary: what this book traces is the continuity of a community adapting to change in an independent manner.

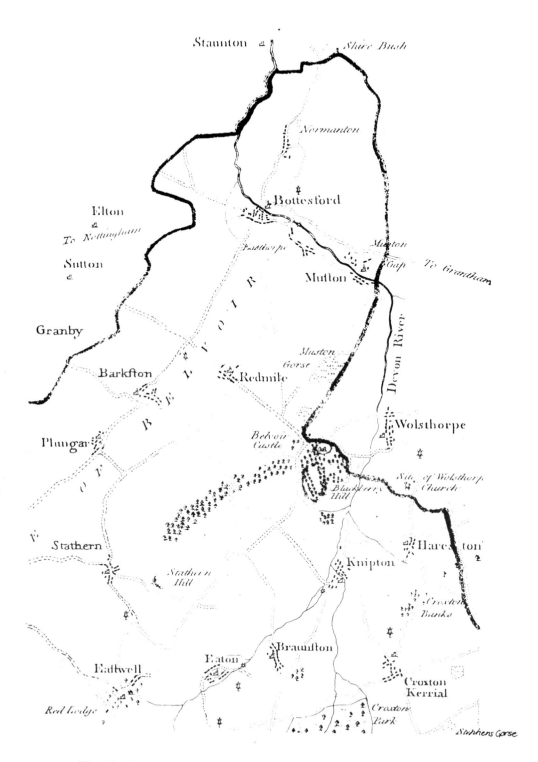

The Northeast corner of Leicestershire from John Prior's map 1777.
(LAO)

12

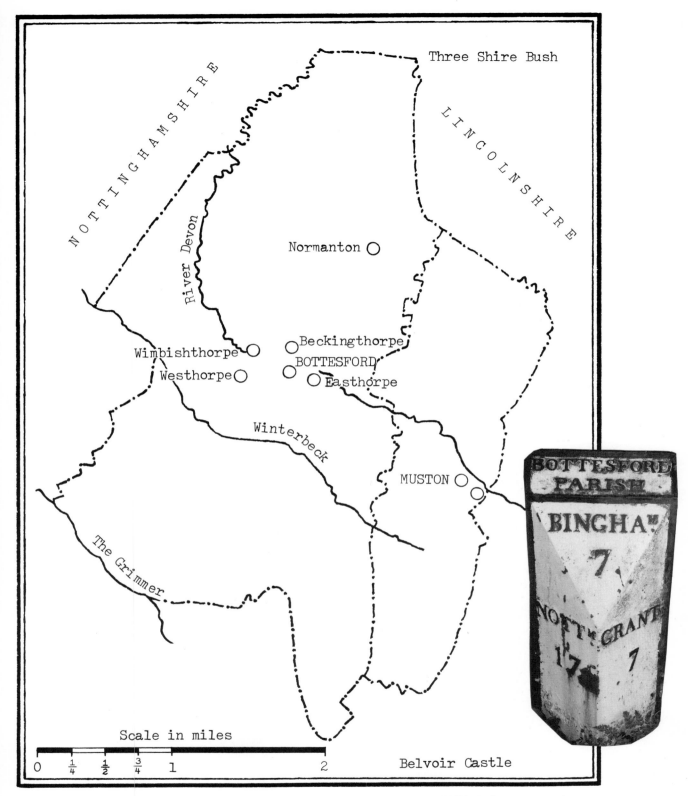

Bottesford and Muston Parishes. (VPE) INSET: Milestone on the
Grantham Road.

13

We were now directed down the Hill into The Vale to Botesford, where I was led to survey the Monuments of The Manners's,[48] and an awkward rugged ride, we found it.—Botesford is a long dirty Village, has a beautiful Church with a very lofty Spire; and the Chancel is fill'd by the magnificent Monuments of The Rutlands; the inspection of which thoroughly, and reading the Inscriptions (particularly that of the two children who perish'd by Sorcery[48] would employ a whole morning: They are beautifully carved in marble. The Parsonage of this rich Living (Mr Thorotons) is now Rebuilding. This Inscription is on a Tombstone in The Church-Yard.

RICHD. WHITACKER

1775

Aged 24 Years.

Our Lifes a Journ'y on a Winters day,
Some only breakfast first, and so away;
Others stay Dinner, and depart well fed,
The longest lived but sup and go to Bed;
Those most in debt who linger out the day,
Who first depart has less and less to pay.

The Road from Botesford thro' new Enclosures was very rough and unpleasant till we reached the Nth Road at Long-Benyngton; whence we rode slowly on over a flat meadowy Country (where were many pastoral shews of milking by maids on their Sundays dress) to Newark.

ABOVE: Bottesford in 1789 from Lord Torrington's diary. (LTD)
BELOW: The Ford leading to the Green c1900. (DB)

Beautiful Bottesford

In November 1941 a slightly homesick Australian bomber pilot, George Hawes, wrote home, ironically describing the newly built aerodrome as 'beautiful Bottesford, the camp à la mud'. As he got to know Bottesford and Muston so he learnt to enjoy the countryside. 'After church we rode all over the countryside around Belvoir Castle through some beautiful woods and wild flowers'. And then 'on Sunday we went for a long bike ride round the old villages for which this country is noted. There is no doubt about the beauty of these places'. But George Hawes was right to stress the mud alongside the beauty, for it derives from the lower lias clay which surrounds the village, providing the outlying soils of the parish which are so good for grain. Along the banks of the Devon in the centre the soil is different, a pebbly sand; this is easy to work, and its combination with the heavier clays close by gives us the basic explanation for the settlement of Bottesford.

The village was built on this site as well because of extensive underground water, into which over the years innumerable wells have been sunk, culminating by 1900 in 98 hand-worked pumps. The sands on which the village is largely built make an awkward subsoil in association with this water, creating a phenomenon known locally as running sand. Tractors have sunk down deep into these and, while the by-pass was under construction in 1988, difficulties were encountered in laying the new road.

However, the by-pass proved an invaluable aid in the search for traces of early settlements. Over the years Roman artifacts have been found, largely to the north of the village, especially in St Mary's churchyard and in the Devon by Rectory Farm. Mr E.A. Shipman has reconstructed a calcite gritted jar found by grave diggers in the churchyard and it is dated 100 BC – AD 60/70 by the Leicestershire Museum Service. Two querns for grinding corn, from similar dates, were found among the Rutland family tombs in the church. A Roman comb on display in the Jewry Wall museum in Leicester was found by village schoolchildren near Rectory Farm. Recently the by-pass excavations, coupled with crop mark studies, have clarified the picture considerably. Iron Age pottery and enclosures, a Roman coin found on the by-pass and quantities of Roman pottery found in an Easthorpe garden complement the churchyard finds. These finds clarify the settlement picture, particularly in association with finds at Staunton, immediately to the north, where an Iron Age farmworker's hut was excavated. Crop markings show Iron Age enclosures on Toston Hill and near the Easthorpe smallholding called California.

Clearly, grain farming was under way across the parish, which must have been cleared for cultivation, if not yet drained, by the beginning of the Christian era.

In addition to archaeological evidence, the study of place names, especially the names of hills, streams and fields, helps to create a picture of the settlement between the Iron Age and the Norman Conquest. There is not the slightest hint of ancient woodland. The few woods today are the relics of fox coverts for hunting. The land was clear, apart from extensive areas of gorse which covered much of Muston. The place name Muston Gorse still survives; there was a gorse for Easthorpe and probably one for Normanton to the north. Gorse was collected for kindling, for lighting bread ovens and cooking fires. Eventually the gorse areas provided cover for rabbits but there were no rabbits until around AD 1000, when they were introduced by the Normans and protected as providers of fur and a high status food.

Perhaps the oldest surviving names relate to the streams; something of the chronology of the settlement emerges from the etymology of river and beck names. The main water course is the Devon, a name which is Celtic in origin and predates the Saxon and Anglo-Danish settlements. It means 'black river', and certainly, if one stands on the wooden bridge by the Church in the evening, the Devon has a distinctly black appearance, although its rate of flow and depth have changed considerably. Parish boundaries became permanent around 800–900, when reorganisation was forced on England by the Danish invasions. The Devon provides a small section of the parish boundary to the north-west. Both the Winterbeck and the Grimmer are used as boundary streams. The name Grimmer could be either Anglo-Saxon or Danish, but Winterbeck suggests a Danish dialect origin. Beck, derived from *bekkr*, Old Norse for a stream, implies a name given to a watercourse which dried up during the summer. The Winterbeck serves as the boundary both to the west and east of the old parish. Another stream name has recently almost disappeared – the Rundle Beck or Runnel, which provided an open drain along the length of the High Street. The name simply means 'small watercourse'.

What this etymological survey shows is that streams were of central significance in the settlement of the area and that it was the Devon which tied together the four settlements of Muston, Easthorpe, Bottesford and Normanton. Streams were used as boundaries wherever possible, but ancient pathways were used too, although most of these are now lost. To the north, the parish boundary, at that point also the county boundary, was clearly marked by Three Shire Bush. The 18th century Leicestershire historian Nichols reports 'at which place, during the perambulations of the parishes, after prayers by the clergymen, were various sports for children'. The most important ancient track to cross the parish was Long Hedge Lane; this provided the boundary between Bottesford and Normanton. The Lane went from Sewstern Lane to cross the Trent at Hazelford Ferry just north of Flintham. A short section still exists in Bottesford, immediately west of the industrial estate to the north. The boundary between Bottesford and Easthorpe was the old track running due south from the Market Cross, now known as Belvoir Road.

This road skirts Toston Hill, an important Easthorpe field. Toston might be derived from the old English *tot-stan*, or look-out stone, and an intriguing, possibly Iron Age enclosure has been identified on top. Nearby Hunger Hill is a post-Conquest name indicating poor fertility. The hill shape to the south used to have the name Huntershorn, a horn-shaped spur, which the canal engineers cleverly used in the 1790s to keep the Grantham Canal on the level. The other major hill in the vicinity is Beacon Hill, or Palmer's Hill as it is called, following the establishment of the Palmer family in the farm to the north of St Mary's in 1902.

Palmer's Hill separates Normanton from Bottesford, suggesting a distinction between the two settlements which is reinforced by the line of Long Hedge Lane. The final and perhaps most conclusive place name evidence comes from the names of the settlements themselves. The form Bottesford is first found as *Botesford*, in Domesday Book of 1086. Other early forms are *Botlesford* in 1125 and *Bodlesford* in 1236. The name is derived from the old English *botl*, meaning a house, which clearly indicates that the post-Roman settlement was a Saxon village. All the later settlements associated with Bottesford – Easthorpe, Wimbishthorpe, Beckingthorpe and Normanton – are derived from Danish settlements in the AD 800–900 period. Easthorpe means the hamlet to the east. Wimbishthorpe means the hamlet by the reedy meadow pasture, and Normanton means the settlement of the Northmen. Muston was Saxon, and it probably means the settlement on the muddy or musty stream *ie* the Devon. A possible alternative derivation is from *mus-ton*, or the mouse-infested settlement. Muston folk today are still looking for the mice, which are not widespread!

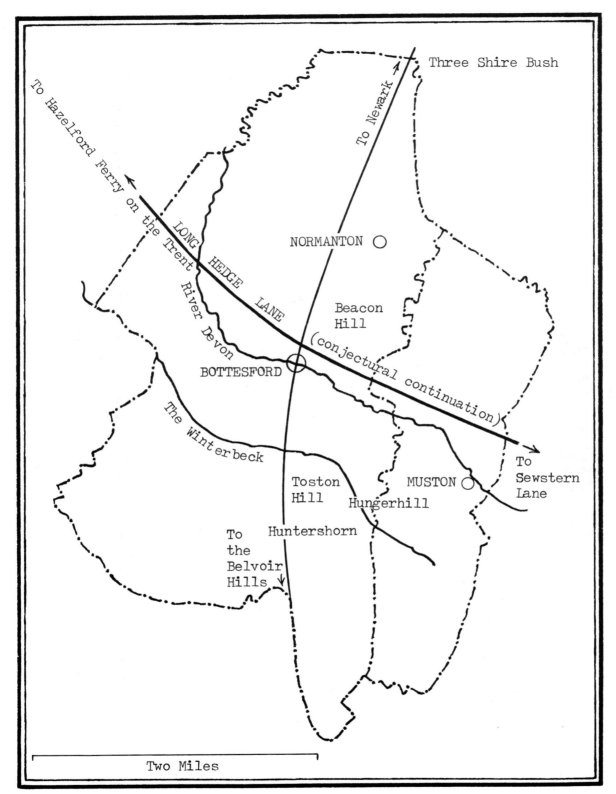

Landmarks and early roads.

17

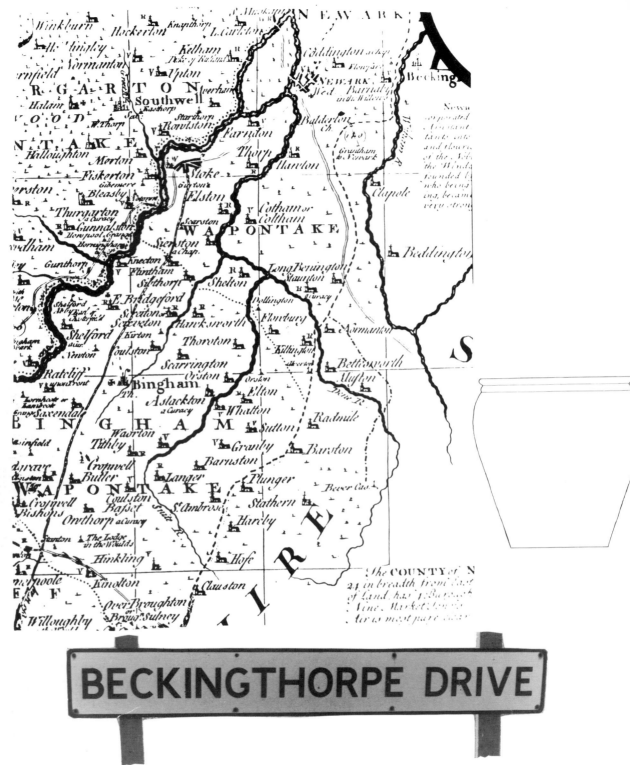

BECKINGTHORPE DRIVE

ABOVE: Emanuel Bowen's map in 1744 shows the line of Long Hedge Lane dotted from Redmile to the Trent; it should be from Bottesford to the Trent. (NRO) RIGHT: Mr E.A. Shipman's reconstruction of late-iron age or early Roman storage vessels, discovered in St Mary's churchyard. (EAS) BELOW: Beckingthorpe Drive.

ABOVE: Cross and Stocks and haystack — the whipping post's iron shackles are clear. (PM) LEFT: The cross garlanded for Armistice Day. (PM) RIGHT: The Stocks were moved in the 1960s. (DB) BELOW. Their present day position (HER) and RIGHT: Stocks, whipping post and Cross and the School. (DB)

ABOVE LEFT: Nichols' view of the Muston Cross in 1792 (JN) and RIGHT: The Cross reconstructed in the 20th century. (JN) CENTRE: Robert de Todeni's stone coffin in Belvoir Castle. (JN) BELOW LEFT: Seal of William de Albini from Nichols (JN) and RIGHT: Lady Margaret de Roos (d1439), in St Mary's Church. (JN)

The Landowners

The Domesday Book entry for Bottesford is extraordinary. Not only does it give the name of the Anglo-Danish lord of the manor, Leofric, and the new Norman lord in 1086, Robert de Todeni, it also gives the name of six French soldiers of fortune and four unnamed compatriots who crossed with Robert to do battle at Hastings in 1066. The six, named Odard, Baldric, Clarebald, Robert, Heldwin and Gilbert, were given land in the parish of Bottesford along with four other *francigeni*, by Robert de Todeni, who became the Lord of Belvoir. As one of William's greatest barons, Robert was granted estates in 11 counties in England, including manors in 35 Lincolnshire and 16 Leicestershire parishes. This is the origin of the huge Belvoir estate, of which Bottesford was by far the largest parish.

Leofric, Robert de Todeni's predecessor, was probably named after Earl Leofric, the last great Mercian Earl, whose widow, Lady Godiva, was still alive in 1066, holding land in Newark. Leofric also held Woolsthorpe and Stathern. It is unlikely there was any real fortification at Belvoir before Robert de Todeni. It was he who constructed the castle and then gave smallholdings in Bottesford to his castle guard of knights and sergeants, the ten *francigeni* of Domesday Book. In exchange for castle guard, they were each granted estates of between 100 and 200 acres. Another member of the castle guard was Mauger, who was granted the small manor of Staunton, immediately north of Bottesford. Mauger's descendant, Mr Edmund Staunton, still carries out his feudal duty of supplying a bell rope for Bottesford so that a warning bell to summon the castle guard can be rung. Robert de Todeni came from the tiny hamlet of Tosny in Normandy, on the Seine south east of Rouen. He was the lord of Bottesford, where at least 1,000 acres were held by 60 Anglo-Norman freeholders and 17 semi-free smallholders. His demesne farm of around 50 acres was worked by six slaves. In around 1077 Robert founded Belvoir Priory, at the bottom of the northern slopes of the castle ridge. When he died, after 1086, he was buried at the Priory.

We know a little about two of the *francigeni*. Baldric was probably Robert de Todeni's steward, a knight of significance, who also held other manors from Robert. Odard was the founder of the de Hotot family which gradually came to dominate the parish, along with the de Saxendale and the de Huntingdon families, all of whom are listed in 1215 among the Knights and the Sergeants guarding the castle against King John. Odard presumably came from Hotot en Auge, a tiny Normandy village on the River Dives, south of Dives-sur-Mer, whence William the Conqueror set sail in 1066. It is possible to trace the family's fortunes through three centuries in and around the parish. Their Bottesford estate was at its height in 1308, when it was granted by Margery and John de Hotot to their son Ralph for a rent to them of a rose flower yearly, at the feast of the nativity of St John the Baptist. This Ralph was a descendant of the first Bottesford person of whom we have a likeness, Ralph de Hotot, who flourished in the twelfth century. Charters show the whereabouts of the de Hotot land, scattered throughout the open fields of Muston and Bottesford.

21

The family witnessed innumerable charters of land sales throughout the period 1150 to 1350, coming to a climax around 1300. In 1342 there is a complex land sale by the Hotot family, witnessed by John Hottow, of land 'in diverse places lying in the field of Botulesford' to William Cooper. But this is the last charter with their name and in 1348 the Black Death swept through England. The final reference to the de Hotots is in the 1381 Poll Tax return for Bottesford, where John Hothoo, husbandman, and Alice his wife paid a 3s charge, higher than the average 1s, but lower than their original knightly status would have warranted.

A second family who witnessed many land exchanges was the Wimbish family. Probably they originated from Bottesford itself, as the north-western part of the village towards Rectory Farm, by the Devon, was originally known as Wimbishthorpe. The name was spelt in many different ways: Wynebis, Wyndon, Winebis or even Wimby. During the 13th century William, son of John of Winebis of Bottesford, witnessed a charter granting a strip of 'arable land in the west field of Botlesford, lying upon Clayholmfurlong, between the land of Thomas de Holtot and that of Robert de Huntedone'. In 1236 Thomas de Winesbise paid 3s 4d as a feudal aid or tax demanded from significant local landowners, on the marriage of Henry III's sister Isabel to Frederick, King of the Romans. Roger de Hotot paid 6s 8d towards the same feudal aid, the highest assessment in the parish. 100 years later those families paid the same assessment of 8s in the 1332 lay subsidy. The family continued to witness charters through the 14th century, but again the 1381 Poll Tax appears to record a dramatic decline in their fortunes as John Wymbish was a ploughman, paying 1s, the routine amount for a working person.

Highlighting the Hotot and the Wimbish families illustrates the rise of landed families, which coincided with the dramatic population explosion in England during the 300 years after the Conquest. In fact Bottesford was the fourth largest settlement in Leicestershire at the beginning of the 14th century, following Leicester, Melton and Wigston. Then came the famines of the early 14th century, the result of heavy population pressure. But at least plenty of men were available to work the land. However, the outbreak of plague which struck Western Europe in 1348 with unparalleled ferocity changed the nature of Bottesford. Gradually land holdings were deserted, so much so that in 1440 22 smallholdings were worthless for they were 'ruinous'.

The parish coped by the nationwide expedient of shifting the delicate balance of farming emphasis from arable to sheep. This small but significant shift can best be studied by a careful analysis of the manorial holdings of the highest status families in Muston and Bottesford. The Lords of Belvoir maintained their Manor of Bottesford with their manor house in Easthorpe. The Lords of Castle Bytham, the Colville family who held Bytham from the Count of Aumale, also possessed manorial lands in Muston and Normanton. The term manor means a distinct, limited area of land consisting (usually) of a main dwelling house (or capital messuage), a private demesne farm, and land in the open fields and pasture let to tenants in return for services or rent. The Lords of Belvoir's capital messuage can be studied in detail as the site in Easthorpe is still clear and the de Roos family crest still adorns the wall of the manor house. The Colville manor house in Muston was almost certainly on or near the site of Hospital Farm. This can be deduced from two pieces of evidence. Around 1360, following the Black Death, and doubtless reflecting the mood of sombre introspection and self-inflicted chastisement which was the response to that catastrophic phenomenon, the Colvilles granted their Muston manor to Owston Abbey near Burrough Hill in Leicestershire. There are extensive earthworks associated with Hospital Farm which seem like fish ponds, suitable for supplying a monastic establishment. After the reformation the Owston lands passed to the Lords of Belvoir and the Muston estate was used to endow the Men's Hospital in Bottesford, which explains the name, Hospital Farm.

The de Roos Manor of Bottesford was well documented, with three especially good descriptions in 1285, 1343, and 1440. Money rentals were increasing up to 1343; the small holders paid £11 3s 4d in 1285 and £26 in 1343. By 1440 these rentals had all but disappeared and the 20 smallholdings brought in no income. Population pressure and decline is revealed by the changing income from the village oven provided by the Lord of the Manor. In 1285 the Lord received £1 10s 0d from the smallholders and labourers for their baking. In 1343 two ovens earned £2, but by 1440 the income had diminished to 11s from one oven. The income from mills diminished from £3 in 1285 to £2 6s in 1343, down to £1 from the Easthorpe water mill in 1440. This reflects a cut in grain production, which is clearly revealed by the difference between the relative value of arable land on the one hand and meadow and pasture on the other. By 1440 meadow land was worth 2s an acre and arable only 8d: hay and pasture for stock was a more profitable farming investment than corn for consumption. Sheep and beasts provided wool, leather and meat and some surplus for market. The production of corn with its low yields due to weeds, poor drainage and lack of fertilisers had been heavily labour-intensive and so sheep farming was developed, requiring only a few shepherds.

The static production of corn is revealed as well by the reduction in the number of mills, although improving technology could account for this. There were six mills in Bottesford in 1086 and these were reduced to two water mills by the 17th century. By that time Muston was reduced to one water mill: the Colvilles originally had two, one of which was granted to the Owston Abbey. This second water mill was Sedgebrook Mill, just across the county boundary today but, being west of Sewstern Lane, it was used more by Muston. The mill helps highlight a second Muston family: the Charnells. Like the de Hotots in Bottesford, the Charnells held part of a knight's fee in Muston in exchange for military service at Belvoir Castle. This was no sinecure: in 1215 the 'famous knight' (as Nichols called him), Hugh de Charnells, was in command at Belvoir Castle when he had to take the fateful decision to surrender to King John, rather than hold out for the Barons, in the year of Magna Carta. A deed of 1360 explains how Gilbert Charnells leased land from Owston Abbey which consisted of a 'marshy close and water mill at the end of the town next to the capital messuage of the said Gilbert and a cottage with its croft next to the cross in the town'. This passage explains the present shape of Muston, with its north end towards Hospital Farm, then under Colville influence, close to the manor house, and its southern section around the Cross, clearly in the Charnells' sphere of influence.

The Colvilles' land stretched in a north-westerly direction towards Normanton. The slope due north of the present railway line, as it enters the railway station, was originally Colville land, the name corrupted into Calving Hills by 1770. The Colvilles had a small manor in Normanton of around 170 acres, with a capital messuage which they had given to the Knights of the Temple. The tenant who held the manor in 1288 still had to pay 2s 6d castle guard to the Lord of Belvoir, and 4s to the Knights of the Temple. By 1370 the income of the Normanton manor was still sufficient for the Colvilles to endow two chaplains at Owston Abbey. But by 1436 one of the Colvilles 'piously considering the smallness of the manor of Normanton, the proceeds of which are not sufficient for the pay of one competent chaplain after deducing expenses, has exonerated the Abbot and Convent from finding one chaplain'. This decline of the Normanton Manor also hints at a reduction in arable activity in the century after 1350.

Information about land holding between 1086 and 1500 is derived from charters, which created legal possession of land. In theory, after 1066 all land belonged to the Crown; in practice the only direct interest of the Crown was the military service for which land was the reward and, increasingly, the financial taxation which replaced this knight service. Exactly the same situation is reflected in miniature in Bottesford. The Charnells, the Colvilles, the Hotots, the Wimbishes all theoretically rented their land in return for military service to the Lords of Belvoir; in practice they treated it as their freehold to alienate or sell to whom they wished. This they did in spite of legal prohibition by statute: complex legal forms enabled landowners to avoid breaking the law. There were continuous exchanges and sales of quite small pieces of land. When William Wigston, a Leicester merchant, bought 120 acres in Bottesford, at least 50 land sales had been witnessed in the estate between 1150 and 1500. Land in Bottesford and Muston alienated to Belvoir Priory between 1080 and 1530 is described in 35 charters, and again this is an estate of certainly less than 300 acres. These charters survive because of their charitable , ecclesiastical or territorial nature, but they recreate the reality of six or seven hundred years ago.

Belvoir Priory's land eventually all reverted to the Lord of Belvoir when Henry VIII and Parliament dissolved the monasteries. During its heyday the Priory provided an annual fair; the monks prayed for the souls of the families of its benefactors and offered expert medical help and charitable aid in the form of a dole of bread from the Priory door. At the dissolution the Lords of Belvoir, now the Manners family, also received Owston Abbey lands. It is these two huge accessions to their lands which enabled the family to double their estate in Bottesford from the 1,000 acres of 1086 to the 2,300 acres held at the time of the Enclosure of Bottesford in 1770. The Manners family have always taken their proprietorial responsibilities seriously, and there can be no doubt that the dissolution had positive consequences for Bottesford. The Castle took over the charitable provision of a dole from its gates. While this has not survived, the other major charitable activity, the provision of services for old people, is still carried out. The Owston Abbey lands of some 300 acres in Muston, plus some 40 acres of land in Bottesford, were put in trust by the Countess of Rutland in the 1590s for a Men's Hospital. Today some of this land is extremely valuable and the foresight of the Countess had ensured the continued happy retirement in Bottesford of many elderly people.

These then were the major landowners in Bottesford, apart from the Church of St Mary itself. The Rector of Bottesford held glebe land for his Church of approximately 140 acres. In addition, he was entitled to a tenth of the produce of parish land, unless these had been alienated to other ecclesiastical organisations. At the enclosure of 1770 the Rector's tithes were reckoned to be worth a grant of 600 acres. In addition to the Rector, the parish lands supported two chantry priests, who prayed for the souls of Bottesford people at two altars in St Mary's Church. Land and cottages were given for these two chantries in the mid-14th century, during the period of self-mortification Western Europe endured following the plague in 1348. The land with which these chantries were endowed consisted of two smallholdings associated with four gardens, around 100 acres of arable land and 14.5 acres of meadow. It was used at the beginning of the seventeenth century to endow the Women's Hospital.

In the early seventeenth century there died in London a successful but unmarried Alderman, Henry Smith, buried in Wandsworth aged 79. He was a rich salter and he instructed his executor, William Rolfe of London, to buy estates to endow almshouses in his home town of Dorking, Surrey. Quite why the executor settled on an estate of around 130 acres scattered throughout the open fields and meadows of Normanton no one knows. From the deeds of the estate it originally included a water mill on the Devon, which was not fit to be repaired in 1702. The capital messuage was the Dorking Poor Farm immediately north of the churchyard of St Mary's, known today as Church Farm, and owned by Mr K. Greasley.

To complete the story of institutional land-owning in Bottesford, the 18th century chronicler, Nichols, gives tantalising references to the gradual building up of an estate for the benefit of the parish poor. As pastoral farming developed in the 15th and 16th centuries, so many sheep were given, by will, to the parish for a parish stock. As the parish had no corporate status, landowning was something of a problem and so the Tudor Earls of Rutland took it upon themselves to create a poor estate. The Earls leased land to the trustees of the poor; according to Nichols this land came from a range of gifts and it possibly also included Belvoir Priory land, granted by the Earls for this charity. Houses for poorer parishioners were provided; they were completely rebuilt on land leased by the Dukes of Rutland in 1774 and still exist today as the Bunkers Hill Cottages. Income for maintenance of the poor was derived from this estate of around 36 acres, which was in Normanton. Land was also given for a school by Rev Abel Ligonier and Anthony Ravell in the early 18th century. Like the Poor Estate, this was consolidated into an estate in Normanton of 31 acres by the Enclosure Act of 1770.

By the time of enclosure the Dukes of Rutland and the Rectors between them owned 3,000 acres of the 5,000 acre parish. The Duke and the Rector apparently dominated the village; in fact this was not really the case, for 70 freeholders also held land in 1770 and they were, in effect, direct descendants of the 60 freeholders of Domesday. Most of these freeholders were also tenant farmers of the Duke or the Rector. Families such as the Vincents had begun to build up holdings centuries before: in 1446 Thomas Vincent bought 15 acres lying in Wimbyshwong abutting upon the river Devon. He bought it from Hugh Wimbish who no longer lived in the village, as the Wimbish family had gone to Byleston. Francis Vincent in 1770 had an estate of 64 acres in Normanton and Thomas Vincent was the Duke's tenant of the Canal farm of 124 acres in 1837, and still held as a freeholder his father's Normanton estate. William Ravell in 1837 was the Duke's tenant of six acres, the Women's Hospital tenant of 22 acres and had his own smallholding of 33 acres. The land William Wigston bought in 1515 was consolidated into an estate of 123 acres. At the enclosure this land had been used to help support the great Wigston Hospital in Leicestershire. The estate consisted of small cottages at the junction of the Nottingham Road and Orston Lane, and land in Bottesford – Middle Field and Debdale Field, tenanted in 1837 by William Pickworth. In the same year William Daybell, the first of a local dynasty, was tenant of the Dorking Poor Farm. It is these tenant farmers who were the backbone of the village, as they have been from the Conquest to the present day.

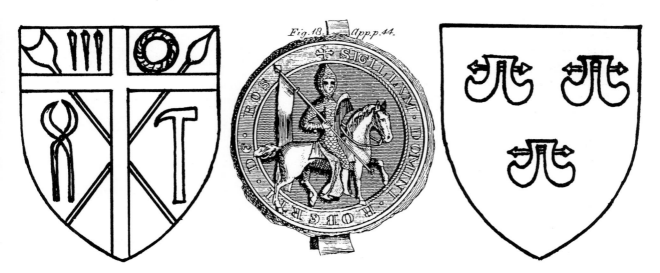

LEFT: A heraldic shield in the West Door of St Mary's; this emblem of the crucifixion suggests there was a Gild of Jesus in Bottesford, to which Ralph Calcraft gave 2s 8d in his will, dated 16 April 1535. (VPE) CENTRE: Seal of Robert de Ros from Nichols. (JN) RIGHT: Heraldic shield of the de Ros family in the West Door of St Mary's; a representation of three sets of two water bags or bottles. (VPE)

25

1381 Poll Tax Returns

Lay Subsidy 133–34, 4 Richard II, 1381

Bottesford – Poll Tax

From Roger Wade, husbandman, 3 shillings
" Thomas Gentil and Joan his wife, husbandman, 2s
" John Holm, husbandman, 12d
" Edith Long, spinner, 4d
" Thomas Brothum and Alice his wife, husbandman, 2s 6d
" John Goos and Joan his wife, husbandman, 2s 6d
" William Assewell and Joan his wife, husbandman, 2s
" William Dynnys, husbandman, 6d
" John Aennycourt and Emma his wife, butcher, 2s
" Alice Assewell, 12d
" John Bele and Alice his wife, husbandman, 2s
" John Baas and Isabel his wife, husbandman, 12d
" John Olyve, husbandman, 12d
" John Gardinir and Joan his wife, husbandman, 2s 6d
" George Gardinir, butcher, 6d
" William Townhende, cobbler and Cecily his wife, 2s
" John Way and Beatrice his wife, husbandman, 3s
" William Heyne and Isabel his wife, 12d
" John Wymmack, Wright and Joan his wife, 18d
" Thomas Assewell, husbandman and Agnes his mother, 12d widow 12d
" Hugh Walker and Alice his wife, 2s
" Nicholas Tailor and Margery his wife, 2s
" Robert Milner, 12d
" John Burgeys, husbandman, 12d
" William Palfreyman, 4d
" Thomas Sele and Cecily his wife, husbandman, 2s
" William Stoke and Alice his wife, husbandman, 2s 6d
" John Assewell and Rose his wife, husbandman, 2s
" Thomas Smyth and Dionisia his wife, husbandman, 2s
" Roger Lucet, husbandman, 12d
" Isabel Lucet, husbandman, 12d
" John, her servant, ploughman, 12d

" William Mortyne, husbandman and Matilda his wife, 2s
" Joan Caunton, husbandman, 5s
" Walter, her son, 4d
" Thomas Colman, husbandman and Jane his wife, 2s 6d
" John, his servant, ploughman, 6d
" Thomas Saxondale, husbandman and Sarra his wife, 2s 6d
" John Godefelawe, husbandman and Isabel his wife, 2s
" Hugh Chapman 4d
" Robert Cook, shepherd, 12d
" John Wyom, husbandman and Alice his wife, 2s
" Matilda o'the chambre, 6d
" Philip Gurney, husbandman and Margery his wife, 2s 6d
" Henry his son 6d
" William Agasson, deyster and Margery his wife, 2s
" Emma his daughter, 12d
" William atte Lane, husbandman and Alice his wife, 2s
" Hamund atte Hall, husbandman and Emma his wife, 40d
" John Hothoo, husbandman and Alice his wife, 3s
" John Kytteson, husbandman, 2s
" Roger Smyth and Alice his wife, 3s
" John Bate, wright and Joan his wife, 12d
" John Lanke, tailor and Joan his wife, 2s
" Agnes Deye, 12d
" John Copp, husbandman and Beatrice his wife, 2s
" William Botheton, husbandman and Matilda his wife, 2s
" Isabel Gurney, widow, 12d
" Alice Syston, webster, 12d
" Margery Olyve, 12d
" John Wymbysh, ploughman, 12d
" John Couper, shepherd, 12d
" John Johnston, husbandman and Alice his wife, 2s
" Robert Stathern, husbandman and Alice his wife, 18d
" John Milner, 8d
" From William Payforall 6d

Sum of persons £160
Sum of Subsidy £8 0s 6d

1837 Bottesford Landowners

Landowner	Arable land	Pasture land			
Duke of Rutland	1139	1358	George Fillingham	–	62
The Rector of			Men's Hospital		
Bottesford	362	406	Trustees	18	40
Richard Bartram	23	61	Thomas Handley	–	11
Joseph Boswell	16	–	Robert Padgett	–	16
Bottesford School			George Fleeman	–	16
Trustees	30	–	Thomas Pickering	–	8
Catherine Bockin	4	6	John Lord	–	10
Dorking Poor Trustees	74	68	William Quant	4	13
Thomas Clarke	–	3	Thomas Kirk	–	6
William Hodson	11	6	Wm. Ravell	–	57
Joseph Challands	1	1	Women's Hospital		
John James	30	23	Trustees	–	48
Thomas Whitehead	–	6	Anthony Healey	11	18
John Kettleborrow	34	31	Mary Stafford	–	27
Richard Kettleborrow	–	70	Mrs. Towne	25	93
John Duffin	1	–	Philip Sutton	1	2
Alice Bemrose	12	63	Thomas Johnson	–	3
Robert Dennis	3	5	William Twinbury	–	47
Thomas Marshall	14	23	Thomas Vincent	–	68
Richard Hough	1	2	Ann Huthwaite	–	10
W.F.N. Norton	5	13	Ann Barrand	–	3
John Jackson	–	6	John Cragg	–	51
Joseph Norris	3	9	Hugh Barnsdale	3	–
William Farney	–	3	Robert Bennett	4	20
John Nixon	–	2	John Brewitt	–	3

These figures are not complete as they exclude people with less than one acre and do not list fractions of acres.

Bottesford Parish Arable Land	– 1855 acres
Bottesford Parish Pasture Land	– 2971 acres

The Enclosure Awards

Comparison of Land Ownership, Wigston and Bottesford.

| Size of estate | No. of Proprietors of land | | Acreage | Acreage | % of total acreage | |
	Wigston	Bottesford	Wigston	Bottesford	Wigston	Bottesford
Under 3			ARP	ARP		
acres	14	20	24-1-37	40-0-39	0.8	0.9
3–5 acres	14	8	55-3-16	30-0-37	1.9	0.7
6–10 acres	22	8	161-1-27	65-3-17	5.6	1.5
11–20 acres	17	9	222-0-14	133-0-2	7.7	3.0
21–50 acres	15	13	472-1-32	419-0-7	16.4	9.4
51–100 acres	8	4	619-0-22	257-3-19	21.5	5.8
101–200 acres	4	4	470-0-19	474-3-22	16.3	10.7
200 + acres	3	2	861-0-27	3015-0-0	29.8	68.0
	97	68	2886-2-34	4436-0-23	100	100

These figures are drawn up from the Enclosure Award of Bottesford and from W.G. Hoskins' study of Wigston in Leicestershire, *The Midland Peasant*. Wigston developed far more into a proto-industrial village than Bottesford did. What this kind of comparison ignores is the fact that tenant farmers held extensive farms with virtually complete security of tenure.

ABOVE LEFT: St Mary's, early 20th century. (DB) RIGHT: St Mary's in the 1950s. (DB) BELOW LEFT: Norman dogtooth work in the ironstone; the doorway is 16th century. (VPE) RIGHT: The 1350 bellman. (VPE)

ABOVE: Reminder of the Wyggeston Hospital, and BELOW: The Wyggeston Hospital, Leicester, built partly with rents from Bottesford in the 16th century. (RC)

29

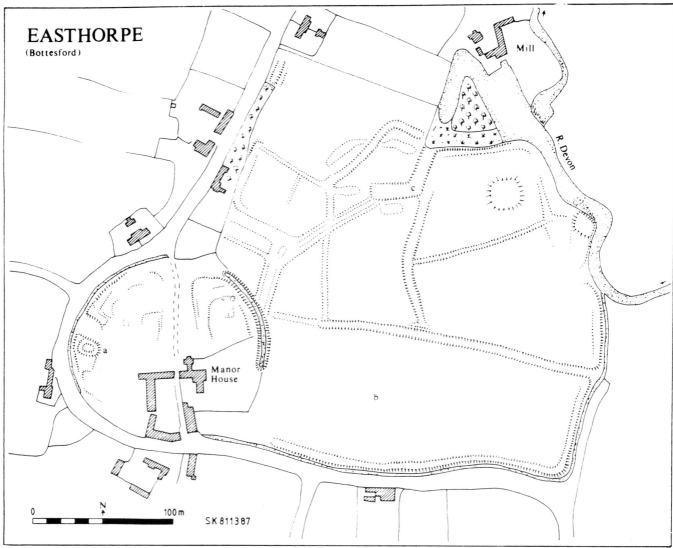

EASTHORPE
(Bottesford)

Mill

R. Devon

Manor
House

0   N   100 m.
                     SK 811387

LEFT: Arms of the Colville family. (JN) RIGHT: Arms of the Charnells
family. (JN) CENTRE: Easthorpe Manor, surveyed by the Leicestershire
County Council archaeological services. The triangular shape is either
fish ponds or a mill pond for Easthorpe Water Mill. (RFH)

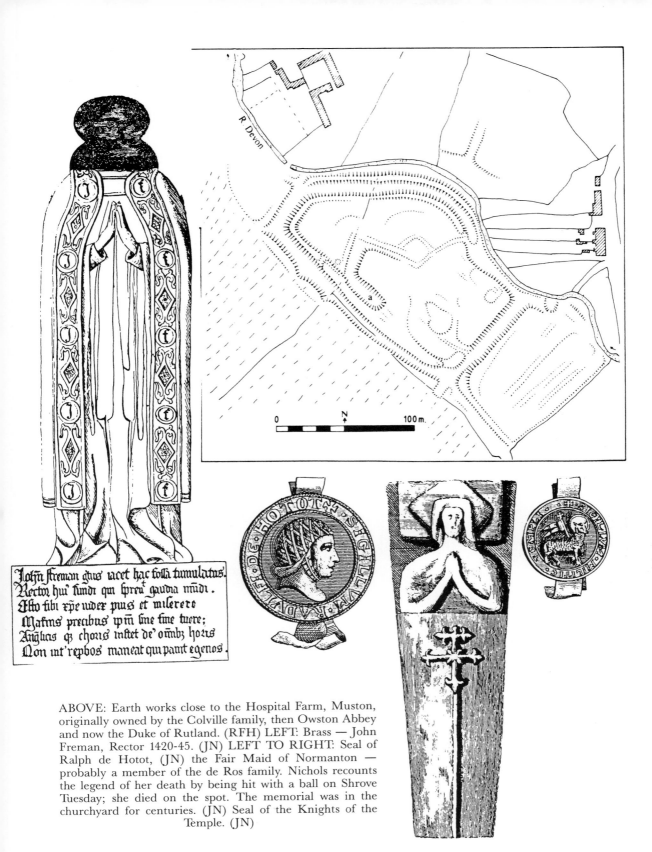

Iohn ƒreman qͫus iacet ħac ƒoſſa tumulatus.
Rectoꝛ ħuͥ ſundi qui ſpreuͭ gaudia mūdi.
Eſto tibi xꝗe iudex piuꝶ et miſerere
Maſinuꝶ precibus ipͫ ſine ſine tuere;
Angliꞑs q̃ chonꝰ inſtet deͦ oͭmbȝ hoꝛis
Qon inͭꝛepꝛobos maneat qui pauit egenos

ABOVE: Earth works close to the Hospital Farm, Muston, originally owned by the Colville family, then Owston Abbey and now the Duke of Rutland. (RFH) LEFT: Brass — John Freman, Rector 1420-45. (JN) LEFT TO RIGHT: Seal of Ralph de Hotot, (JN) the Fair Maid of Normanton — probably a member of the de Ros family. Nichols recounts the legend of her death by being hit with a ball on Shrove Tuesday; she died on the spot. The memorial was in the churchyard for centuries. (JN) Seal of the Knights of the Temple. (JN)

31

Brass — Henry de Codyngton, Rector 1361-1381. (JN)

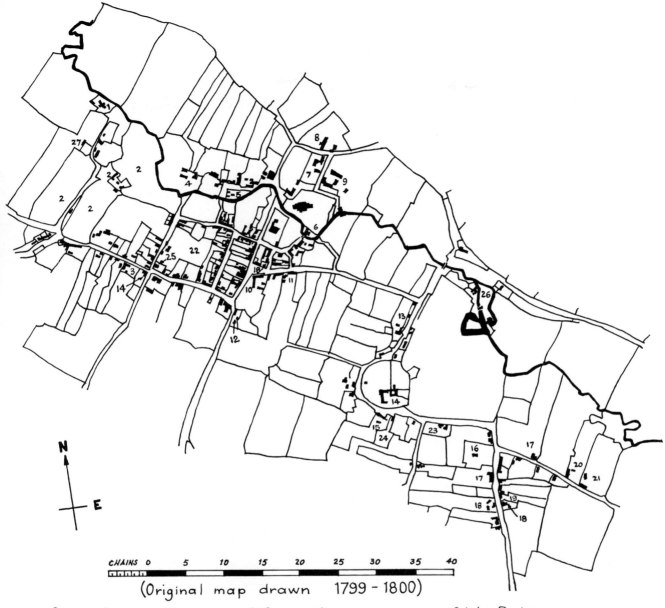

(Original map drawn 1799 - 1800)

1. Rectory Farm
2. The Nook· Moses Calvert
3. Joseph Norris
4. Elizabeth and son, John Kettleborrow
5. Thomas Piggins
6. Jonathan Singleton
7. Richard Bartram
8. William Toddington
9. Dorking Poor

10. Thomas Vincent
11. John Dykes
12. Ann Bull
13. John May
14. Thomas Hough
15. Robert Graves
16. Robert Buxton
17. Francis Lamb
18. John Jervis

19. Wm. Parker
20. Jane Brown
21. John Allam
22. John Wright Surgeon
23. Richard Chambers
24. William Holmes
25. John Lievesley
26. John Ryley
27. Thomas Norris

The villages of Bottesford and Easthorpe: a map produced by
the Agent's office of the Duke of Rutland. Every building in
the village was marked on the map, but not all belonged to
the Duke. All we have listed belonged to the Duke, except for
Rectory Farm. (VPE)

LEFT: The bypass destroyed this small moat-like feature near Hospital Farm in Muston. It was probably a duck decoy. (RFH) ABOVE: Hospital Farm, Muston — a large, dated grain barn still used for its original purpose. BELOW: Poultry have always figured extensively in inventories of local farms. These geese are kept by Mr K. Greasley today, by the Devon. (BH)

Farmers and Tenants

'On the Duke of Rutland's estate ALL are tenants at will, who, notwithstanding, hand down the possession to their posterity: the widow succeeds the husband and not the son, till her death or marriage.' In these words, written in 1792, John Nichols explained the reality of farming in Bottesford. Although most parish land until 1920 was owned by outsiders, in effect the tenant farmers held their land almost as a freehold. By the seventeenth century 21 year leases prevailed on the Men's Hospital Farm and the Dorking Poor estate and, as with the Duke's land, women often held them. Mrs Elizabeth Cam was the tenant farmer of the Dorking Farm in 1702. A 21 year lease was granted to Richard Ward for the Men's Hospital Farm in 1689. The Wyggeston Hospital Trustees still preferred the lease for three lives: Anthony Vincent held about 15 acres of the trustees for three lives in 1656. He nominated two other people alive at the time and the lease lasted till the death of the third, potentially a new long lease.

Tenant rights were strong then in Bottesford, even among the tenants at will, theoretically liable to eviction at any time during the 7, 14, or 21 year leases. The Belvoir Agent was on hand to keep a check on good or bad farming and so the tenancy at will suited them. The institutional landlords at Dorking or Leicester granted cheaper, longer leases as they wanted 'a steady return for a minimum of management costs'. The great advantage of tenancies at will was the opportunity available of waiving a year's rent if times were bad – and the fact that the Belvoir estate did do this reconciled tenants to the theoretical uncertainty of their tenures. As T.W. Beastall wrote in *The Agricultural Revolution in Lincolnshire*, once a system for compensating tenants for their outlays was established, that made annual tenancies at will preferable to leases for both landlords and occupiers.

The land, then, was farmed either by a relatively small number of owner-occupiers, or by the great majority of tenant farmers. One of the Duke of Rutland's principal tenants was Mr Hand. In 1799 John Hand had 32 acres but soon he moved in to the Manor House in Easthorpe, or Hall Farm, which the Hough family had held for years. This major farm of 273 acres now became the site of Hand's sheep-breeding experiments. Eventually he produced prize-winning rams by crossing the old breeds with the new breeds developed by Robert Bakewell. Mr Hand was the Duke's largest tenant farmer at the beginning of the 19th century; his family is still remembered in Hand's Walk and the bungalows on the site of Hand's Almshouses in High Street.

Among the other major tenant farmers in 1799, Moses Calvert held a farm of 134 acres: Nook Farm, off Pinfold Lane. Elizabeth Kettleborrow had a farm of 113 acres with her son John: this is Devon Farm, today owned by the Taylors. William Toddington had 137 acres in Beckingthorpe, John Dykes farmed 90 acres known as the Canal Farm, later the Daybell Farm, opposite the Red Lion, and Thomas Vincent held the second largest farm, 211 acres, now Acacia Farm. Richard Bartram farmed 147 acres of the Duke's land at Beckingthorpe Farm.

The principal farm in Easthorpe was held by Francis Lamb on the western side of the village street. Further towards the Castle, John Jervis farmed 91 acres which is now Sands Farm. In Normanton, women farmers were dominant in 1799. Susannah Spreckley farmed 100 acres and Mary Guy 102 in the hamlet, where the largest tenant farmer was John Bockin, with John Cragg farming 137 acres. These figures show that the size of the larger tenant farms of the 18th and 19th centuries was generally between 100 and 250 acres, with the farmhouses firmly in the centre of the built-up areas.

This concentration of farmhouses at the centre of the village had developed from the open field system, when tenants had land scattered throughout the parish. The tenants themselves organised the farming year, not having a dominant resident squire: the family at the Castle showed a benevolent interest but left to the steward or agent any direct interference, and the agent was concerned equally with at least 20 other manors. Absentee landlords like the Knights Templar, the Wyggeston Hospital and the Dorking Poor Trustees could not interfere. The only controlling device was the manor court, which survived as the court leet, responsible for drainage inspection, well into the 20th century.

The major problem was lack of effective drainage. The heavy clays were difficult to work, although the natural drainage offered by the Devon, Winterbeck and the Grimmer helped. A 1343 survey clearly shows the tough reality of early farming: on William de Roos' manor there were 208 acres of arable land of which 160 could be sown each year, the rest having to lie fallow. But of the 160, 55 had been sown with winter seed and 20 with peas – in effect apparently not all arable land was actually put under the plough. There were 60 acres of meadow, worth double the arable land per acre but even this was not satisfactory: it was worth 60s and no more, 'because it is dry and poor growing land'. So the Winterbeck clearly did dry up in summer. In addition to the meadow 'there are also different pieces of pasture'.

The map of the open field system reconstructed from the enclosure award clarifies the pattern of early farming. Arable land was probably at its greatest around 1200–1300, when the charters show extensive dealing in sections of such land. Thomas and Robert de Hotot, Robert Huntingdon and William de Wynebis witnessed a transfer in the 13th century to Alan or Bottesford, chaplain, of 'four selions of arable land in the field of Bottesford, whereof one selion lies in *le Sandes* upon the furlong called *Hardhilles*'. In other words the land is hard work. The extraordinary way in which the arable strips were spread out all over the fields is revealed in the 1675 description of the Dorking Poor estate, which had 167 parcels or strips of land spread out all across the arable, meadows and pasture. The Wyggeston estate of less than 150 acres was split between 10 smallholders in 1656 and 12 in 1687. By that time much arable land was being put down to pasture.

Hints of the shift from arable to pastoral farming are contained in the 1381 poll tax return, which shows shepherds, and several people earning their living from spinning, weaving and dyeing. Sheep pasture is clearly marked on the open field map. It is intriguing to note the number of butchers in the village then: this shows there was enough work to employ two people full-time killing animals – today there are three butchers. Each family had its own cows by the 17th century; Robert Pecke held a house of the Wyggeston trustees in 1656, which had two cow pastures attached. George North's cottage had the right to pasture for two cows and 10 sheep and Richard Tutbury's cottage, which he held on a lease of three lives, entitled him to pasture for 2.5 cows and ten sheep. Extensive sheep farming had developed by the 16th century, as is apparent from wills of the time. In 1588 Mr Hutton, the parson, bequeathed '80 sheepe; which my will is, that they shall be ordered in their sort: that is to say, yerely letten to four honest poore men within the parish of Bottisford'.

So gradually land was being taken out of tillage and put down to pasture. It also appears that woodland was encouraged; a manorial inquest on the Bottesford Manor in 1483 reveals

20 messuages, 10 tofts, 300 acres of (arable) land, 40 acres of meadow and 200 acres of wood. The wood must have had two functions, firstly for fruit, since the area became well known for damsons, plums and apples, and secondly wood for timber was encouraged. It was proving too difficult to work arable land due to the post-Black Death population drop, to the difficulties of drainage and also to the expense of manuring land. So sheep were put on the far pastures, which were taken out of cultivation.

The biggest change to pasture took place during the 17th and 18th centuries as the Manners family began to extend and consolidate their holdings in the parish. The object was enclosure of land for grazing. Hedging and fencing was not a problem in Bottesford since most of the land belonged to the Belvoir Estate anyway. The real problem was one of improving it by drainage. Extensive meadow and pasture lands to the west and north-west of the parish were carefully managed by drainage, certainly by the early 18th century. This water management was a facet of England's agricultural practice vital to the feeding of a growing population in the 18th century.

Today's Cambridge botanist, Oliver Rackham expresses the change nicely: 'after 1500 there came the growth of that supreme technical achievement of English farming, the irrigated water meadow'. In Bottesford the Devon was dammed just where it flowed from Bottesford into Normanton, near the old Long Hedge Lane crossing. Water was then introduced into a new drain which ran to an extensive 'reservoir or watering place' in the middle of the Normanton fields called Chippendale. The drain then ran north to join up again with the Devon in two places north and south of the old Mary Bridge. By 1770 the enclosure award described the drain: 'a water course goes from Devon Dam to Chippendale watering place for water and to prevent floods along the line of the water course during wet seasons.' We do not know today if the meadows were actually flooded. This technique became widespread in the 18th century as a means of fertilising the land at the end of winter. A river, preferably one which took sewage from a township, was allowed to flood fields in March, to ensure a fast and lush growth of grass in the spring. A 19th century engineer engaged in this kind of work preferred heavily polluted water, comparing 'the water which is unpolluted to small beer, but when full of sewage to real ale'. The Rundle Beck ran along the High Street of Bottesford and thus might have taken some of the township's sewage into the Devon, perhaps to be spread over the Normanton Meadows.

Whether or not there were actual water meadows must await further research. What is clear is that the 1770 Enclosure Act was the occasion for the most extensive drainage works right across the parish; drainage dykes were constructed or improved and this involved the building of 11 bridges, many of which still survive. This extensive engineering involved an 'arch brick tunnel under the Devon for draining Normanton meadows and pasture into the Winterbeck'. There can be no doubt as to the function of the Bottesford Enclosure Act. Nichols said in 1792 'much of the land has been converted to the purposes of grazing'. As William Pitt wrote in the *Agriculture of the County of Leicester* (1809): 'as in consequence of an increased population, and the increasing riches and luxury of the county, a greater quantity of hay and other produce of grass land is wanting to support a more numerous livestock than formerly, it behoves everyone interested and concerned, to endeavour to extend the breadth of water meadow, as a source for supporting a larger livestock and [thus] raising more manure for improving the upland, by artificial irrigation'.

Pitt also explains the second style of artificial drainage, relics of which can be seen throughout the parish. This was ridge and furrow drainage. 'In the ridge and furrow system the land is laid out in broad ridges with intervening furrows, either by hard work or the plough, and the water is conveyed from a floating gutter at the head of the field into furrows made down the ridges, and spread over the land by paddles placed in the said furrows'.

The change in farming was dramatic: crops were sown in around 6–700 acres only, out of a total of nearly 5,000 acres. This is recorded in crop returns, which are not absolutely reliable, although they were taken for government purposes, associated with the war-time footing of the British economy during the Napoleonic Wars 1793–1815.

Year	Wheat	Barley	Oats	Beans	Total
1793	197	199.5	26.5	144	567
1794	219	191	42	160.5	612.5
1795	314	174	58.5	145.5	692
1801	206.25	162	87.75	175	658

What the figures offer is proof of the pastoral bias of Bottesford farming, which lasted until the 20th century. But they also show that, during the 1793–1815 war, there was a temporary increase in grain output. The proof for this lies in the huge grain barns constructed during that war – two in particular bearing the date 1807, and both in 1989 being farmed by members of the Donger family: Hollies Farm in Bottesford and the Hospital Farm in Muston. Both farms were owned by the Dukes of Rutland and clearly, in addition to rebuilding Belvoir Castle, the 5th Duke was prepared to spend extensively on barns for his tenant farms to store their grain.

After the French wars the tendency to pastoral farming continued. In 1837 exact figures are available – 1,855 acres of arable and 2,971 acres of pasture. This shows a major turn-round from the enclosure of 1770, when Bottesford Parish had approximately 2,720 acres arable and 1,820 pasture. By the 19th century Bottesford was established as a grazing parish.

The process of 19th century beast farming is reflected in the details of two farmers: Richard Kettleborrow, who died on 18 September 1857, and Mrs Ann Lovett, who died in 1913. William Welbourn, schoolmaster and parish clerk, drew up the full value of Richard Kettleborrow's estate after the properties were sold. Kettleborrow was a staunch Primitive Methodist and a tenant farmer of the Duke:

Rd Kettleborrow's residue receipts – final statement

1.	Cash in the house	£ 17.	0.	1d
2.	Sale of furniture	£ 397.	19.	7d
3.	Sale of stock beasts, sheep, pigs etc	£ 863.	7.	1d
4.	Implements sold	£ 728.	8.	10d
5.	Grass, straw, hay	£ 193.	19.	9d
6.	Straw sold to Duke after delapidations	£ 16.	1.	0d
7.	Morgage debts not received and interest due	£1465.	19.	4d
8.	Gutridges interest	£ 3.	18.	9d
9.	Tenant right	£ 193.	3.	3d
10.	House sold to Wright	£ 820.	0.	0d
11.	Close sold to Leatherland	£ 293.	16.	9d
		£4993.	13.	8d

Clearly the major revenue from this farm was from stock beasts, which consisted of 67 sheep, 27 beasts, 10 horses and two pigs. Richard Kettleborrow's debts amounted to £4549 8s 3d after all expenses had been paid, leaving a residue of £444 5s 5d. In addition to stock, he kept a great quantity of poultry – geese, fowls, ducks and pigeons. His main crop seems to have been beans: his estate realised £193 for 98 quarters of beans at £1 19s 6d a quarter. £7 5s 6d was received for potatoes. He was a successful farmer and had won prizes worth £20 at successive meetings of the Waltham Agricultural Association. He lived in the village, in the 1850s in the Nook Farm, which was sold at his death, along with other property he owned in the village.

It is also possible to reconstruct the farming operation of Mrs Ann Lovett. Her farm was in Normanton, the last one on the right going north, Rose Cottage in 1989. She had been a tenant of the Duke of Rutland for many years: in 1894 she held the Normanton farm of 122 acres from the Duke and nine acres in her own right. She had four horses and 22 beasts, one of which was a Lincoln Red. She kept 30 poultry, including one cock. She had 31 sheep and 24 lambs. Of her estate only the accounts of the sale of live and dead stock survive – not of the value of the house or the crops. But the following table certainly shows the significance of their stock.

Sale of Mrs Ann Lovett's Live and Dead Stock 1913

Household goods	£ 24.	4s.	0d
Beasts	£207.	18s.	6d
Horses	£ 72.	9s.	0d
Fowls	£ 3.	18s.	9d
Sheep	£ 89.	16s.	0d
Farm implements	£ 44.	0s.	3d
	£466.	10s	6d

The Daybells were a well-known farming family. They came into the village as tenants of the Dorking Poor Farm in 1829, when William Daybell of Balderton, Nottinghamshire, farmer, took over a 21 year lease at a rent of £172 16s 0d per annum. Daniel Daybell, born in 1811, presumably one of William's sons, took out a lease on the Dorking Poor Farm in 1851, again at a rent of £172 16s 0d. He died around 1871 and the farm (now Church Farm) went to William Richard Daybell for a rent of £192. This was reduced to £100 per annum on a yearly tenancy from 1893, giving an indication of the hard times of the 1880s and '90s. But meanwhile Daniel's son, Daniel Richard Daybell, was born in 1840. As a young scholar, he attended the old village school in the churchyard. In 1870 he took over the tenancy of the Duke's Canal Farm, opposite the Red Lion, having farmed since 1860 at the Dorking Poor Farm. He was a champion ploughman, winning many prizes after his first success in 1860 at Bingham, and becoming Champion of All England. He reared foxhounds for the Belvoir Hunt, winning silver cups on two occasions. He acted as steward to the Rector's wife, Lady Adeliza Norman. He was Clerk of the Parish Council from the start of that organisation and, for 40 years from 1889 to 1929, he was clerk of the successor to the manor court, the court leet, responsible for parish drainage. At his funeral in 1930, the coffin of plain oak was 'borne on Mr Daybell's farm dray which was drawn by his favourite horse, and Mr Waudby, a farmer employee, had charge of the vehicle'. His prowess at cricket and singing were made much of in his obituary in the *Grantham Journal*.

Daybell's greatest claim to fame was his extraordinary success as a pig breeder, which brings us back to the pastoral farming of the 19th century. Local cows were used to produce milk which had three basic functions. It was drunk locally and also sent far afield, as soon as effective railway transport became widespread after 1850. Milk provided cream for the Stilton cheese made locally by most farmers. Mrs Lovett had five pancheons, yokes, and churns in her dairy in 1913. But the third by-product was whey, kept for the pigs. Daybell's obituary in the *National Pig Breeders Association Gazette* describes 'a wonderful record of successes at agricultural shows.

At the Royal Show he won no fewer than 174 prizes – a magnificent achievement. For years in succession the first prize for a pair of young boars was awarded to the Bottesford herd and in those successive years Mr Daybell exhibited the champion sow'. Daybell pigs from Bottesford were sold to breeders all over the world. His visitors' book in 1903 shows buyers from South Africa, Ireland, Holland, Sweden and Austria. His first boar came from Mr James, an old Elton farmer, and Daniel exhibited it at Bingham while winning the ploughing match. Daybell's herd book shows endless champions, several called Bottesford Buttercup, many called Bottesford Empress and one called Marchington Queen, a great champion around 1914.

The pigs brought prosperity to the village in general and to the Daybells in particular at a time of farming depression. Thus they partly enabled parish farmers to weather difficulties caused by the enormous growth of imports of foreign corn, and of rent increases at the end of the 19th century. But the major reason for this relative prosperity was the continued reliance on mixed farming. As William Pitt expressed it in 1809, most farms were '80–100 acres where the occupier put their own hands to the plough'. These tenant farmers were prepared to work hard, to manure their land by hand, using dung from animals and pigeons. The relationship between owners, tenants and working men and women was a close one, a relationship often cemented during hunting; the grazing lands of Bottesford were ideal for the Belvoir Hunt, especially during the time of the 6th Duke, a popular Master of the Belvoir from 1857 until his death in 1888. In 1877 the Duke received a set of solid silver candelabra from the 'gentlemen and farmers of the Belvoir Hunt' and he replied saying: 'All classes meet together – the peer, the landowner, the yeoman and the peasant. You see them all enjoy it'.

Inventory of Thomas Calcraft: 1556

In the barne

Item whett (wheat) be estimacion iiij quarters		iiijli	(£4)
Item Rye be estimacion iij quarters		iijli	(£3)
Item Barley be estimacion xxti (twenty) quarters		xvli	(£15)
Item pees (peas) be estimacion iij quarters		xlij	(42s)
Item hay be estimacion		xls	(40s)
Item waine (cart) and plowghe yokes and temes (teams) and geres (gears) belonigng (belonging) to the same	xxxiijs	iiijd	(33s 4d)
Item hovells, pallis (posts) with other wode (wood) in the yeard (yard)	xxvjs	viijd	(26s 8d)

Cattle belonging to the yeard

Frist (first) Oxen iiij		vjli	(£6)
Item iiij Kye (Kine)		iiijli	(£4)
Item ij heffers (heifers)		xxs	(20s)
Item ij calves		viijs	(8s)
Item ij bey (bay) mares with ij foles (foals)		xxs	(30s)
Item j bar mare andj downcolte of v yeers (years) hold (old)		xxxs	(20s)
Item Old Shepe xvj		xxxijs	(32s)
Item lames (lambs) x		xvjs viijd	(16s 8d)
Item Swyne fyve		xs	(10s)

Summa (ie total) = lvjli xs vjd (56. 10s 6d)

40

ABOVE: Mr H. Daybell and Mr A. Salisbury in the 1950s.
(DF) BELOW: Mr Parnham with a Lincoln Red bull. (DB)
RIGHT: Mr Cyril Palmer with another Lincoln Red. (CP)

ABOVE: The de Roos crest on Easthorpe Manor House. LEFT: Mr
Parnham's shire horses in the 1920s. (DB) RIGHT: A shorthorn cow.
(DB) BELOW: Len Palmer with his herd of Friesian cows in the 1950s.
(HER)

42

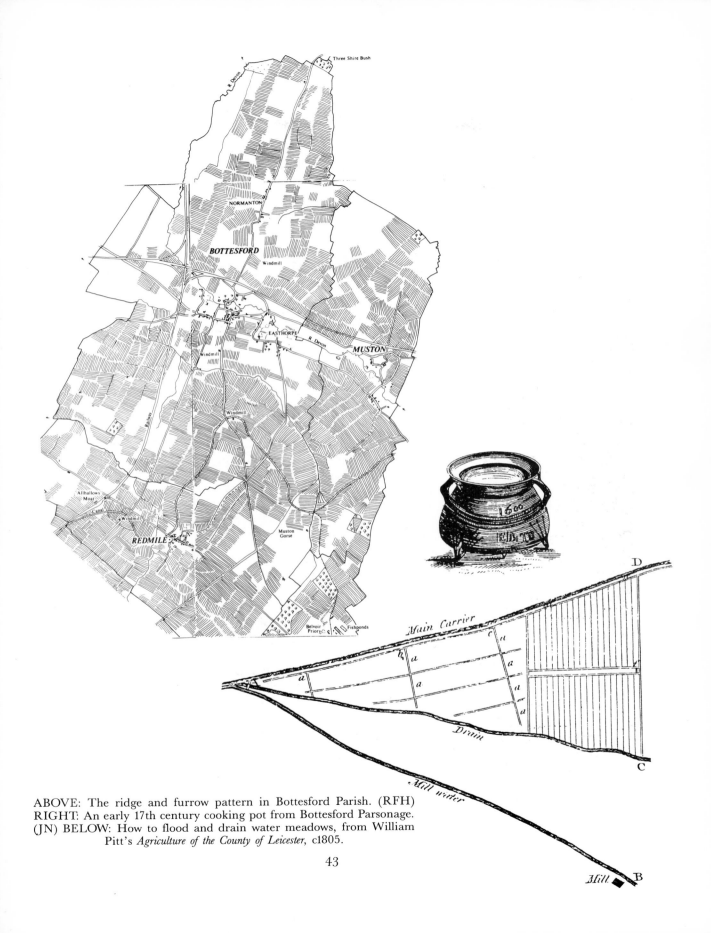

ABOVE: The ridge and furrow pattern in Bottesford Parish. (RFH)
RIGHT: An early 17th century cooking pot from Bottesford Parsonage.
(JN) BELOW: How to flood and drain water meadows, from William
Pitt's *Agriculture of the County of Leicester*, c1805.

43

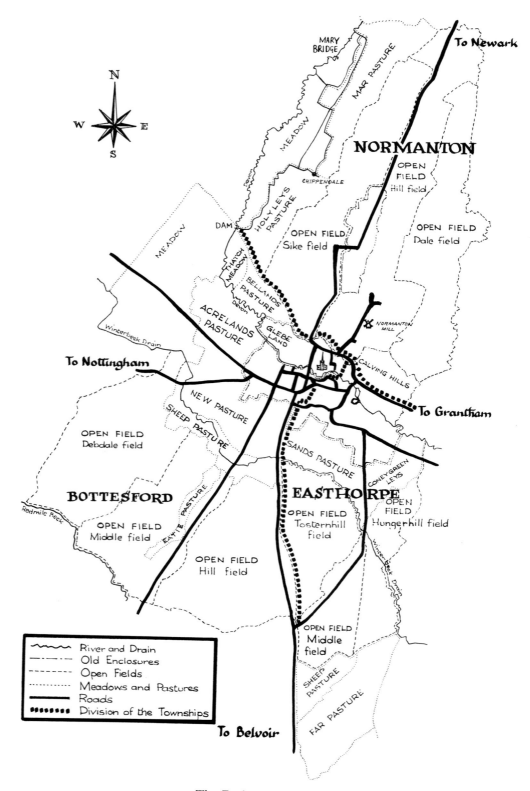

The Enclosure Map. (VPE)

44

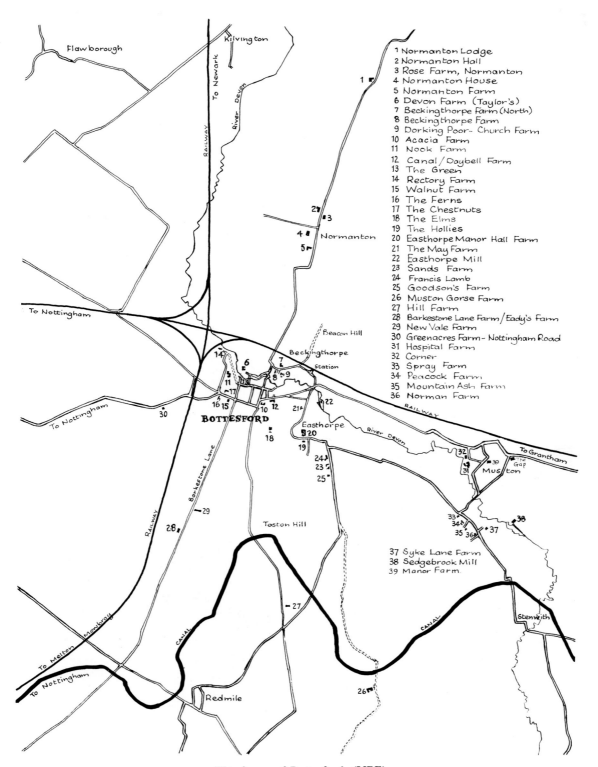

1 Normanton Lodge
2 Normanton Hall
3 Rose Farm, Normanton
4 Normanton House
5 Normanton Farm
6 Devon Farm (Taylor's)
7 Beckingthorpe Farm (North)
8 Beckingthorpe Farm
9 Dorking Poor- Church Farm
10 Acacia Farm
11 Nook Farm
12 Canal / Daybell Farm
13 The Green
14 Rectory Farm
15 Walnut Farm
16 The Ferns
17 The Chestnuts
18 The Elms
19 The Hollies
20 Easthorpe Manor Hall Farm
21 The May Farm
22 Easthorpe Mill
23 Sands Farm
24 Francis Lamb
25 Goodson's Farm
26 Muston Gorse Farm
27 Hill Farm
28 Barkestone Lane Farm / Eady's Farm
29 New Vale Farm
30 Greenacres Farm- Nottingham Road
31 Hospital Farm
32 Corner
33 Spray Farm
34 Peacock Farm
35 Mountain Ash Farm
36 Norman Farm

37 Syke Lane Farm
38 Sedgebrook Mill
39 Manor Farm

The farms of Bottesford. (VPE)

45

Top Mill, Bottesford, by the canal. (LCC)

Day Labour

It is impossible to know if the working people of Bottesford liked being called 'yeoman and peasant'. It is certain that the wide range of crafts derived from agriculture were the main village occupations. In the 18th century, unlike Wigston and Shepshed, Bottesford had 'no stockinger, or other manufacturers, and care taken that there shall be none', or so said the Duke's agent, William King. The objective of the Duke or his agent was simple: it was popularly (and probably correctly) supposed that industrial activity involved frequent unemployment. As fashions changed, so demand for the main industrial products – textiles, ribbons, stockings – fluctuated. This left people liable to starvation unless they could be supported by the parish poor law rates paid by the farmers. The Duke was determined to control these rates, which had begun to increase alarmingly during the French Wars of 1793 to 1815, rising from £120 annually before the war to £414 in 1816/17. The technique was simply to encourage pastoral farming and dairying crafts and to actively, and successfully, discourage other industry.

Bottesford had always been a heavily populated village, but trends in population have varied over the years. Statistics relating to 2,330 families in Bottesford between 1610 and 1851 show a phase of population growth related to arable farming between 1610 and 1669. The next 100 years saw some depopulation with the transition to pastoral farming. From the possessions left at death by the wealthier tenant farmers it appears that their flocks of sheep increased on average from 90 to 140 sheep during the first half of the 18th century. This resulted in a drop in population from 870 in 1676 to 772 in 1792. But the 19th century saw a complete reversal of these figures as population boomed all over England. That of Bottesford increased by 60%, from 804 in 1801 to 1,374 in 1851. This change has been ascribed to the shift away from fattening and grazing, to labour intensive dairy farming, particularly the making of Stilton cheese.

It is also the result of healthier times. Bottesford had suffered badly from plague in the early 17th century, leading to a comment in the parish register in 1610 that 'the dying poisoned many, Th' infection was so great whereat it came, it scarce left any'. In 1610, 125 died; then the average number of deaths in a year was 25. Bottesford recovered and indeed increased in population by the end of the 17th century: the London plague of 1665 seems not to have affected it. But that scourge of the 18th century, smallpox, took its toll, and helps account for a population fall. Nichols attributed 20 out of 45 deaths in 1741 to smallpox. This outbreak seems to have happened shortly after some years of high mortality. There were more than double the annual average of deaths in 1720, 1727, 1728, 1729, 1730 and 1739. From this emerges a somewhat depressed community around 1740, for the expansion of sheep farming cut down grain production. Sheep were then kept more for wool than meat, and the village poor must have suffered serious food shortages, reducing their resistance to disease. A hint of trouble lies in Nichols' statement, written in 1792, that 'Forty years ago [1752] were in this parish 15 public houses, now [1792] but 3; and such is the regularity of the place, that near 800 inhabitants with a turnpike road, would not support these 3, but with the assistance of their respective occupations'. The tenor of Nichols' comments is confirmed by listing the alehouse keepers, inn keepers and victuallers of 1753: Wright Calcraft, William Holmes, Robert Vincent, Thomas Brewit, Randal Kemp, Robert Jarvis, Robert Bennett, John Marshall, Richard Huff (Hough), Thomas Gamble, Jonathan Dykes and Francis Lamb. This went down to nine in 1756, seven in 1757 and five in 1769, and it finally stabilised by 1822 when the following licence holders were recorded: Bottesford – Richard Rowe (or Roe), Rutland Arms; Richard Cooper, Red Lion, and David Hoe, Black Bull or Bull's Head; James Skillington (?) 6 Bells and John Skillington, (?) Marquis of Granby; Belvoir – Robert Shipham, Peacock; Muston – Thomas Ablewhite, Wheatsheaf. The 'regularity of the place' was caused by increasing prosperity resulting from improved agriculture, but it might also have been the result of an evangelical campaign which started in Bottesford during the 18th century with three strong chapels by 1825.

Looking at the village at the time of the crisis in mortality of the 1720s and 30s, it is possible to see why the Duke and his agent (supported by Methodist and Baptist chapelgoers) were anxious to stabilise the parish. These are the names of orphans apprenticed by the parish to learn a trade:

Date	Name of apprentice	Trade to be learnt	Master	Master's Trade
1714	Alice Stevenson	Spinster	William Vincent	Husbandman
1714	Alice Buttle	Spinster	Thomas Summer	Husbandman
1716	William Northly		William Wheatley	Tailor
1717	Mary Bradbery	Spinster	John Warren	Husbandman
1717	Margaret Bradbery	Spinster	Richard Smith	Husbandman
1717	John Handbery	Husbandry	Mr Charles Tomlinson	
1721	John Tarr	Husbandry	William Bennett	
1724	Valentine Bradbury		William Threaves	Framework Knitter
1724	John Bradbury		Samuel Starr	Framework Knitter
1929	Sarah Bradbury	Housewifery Knitting	William Todington	
1729	Bridget Gibson	Spinning Knitting Sewing	Francis Breedon	
1729	Peter Frockingham	Husbandry	Mr Richard Hough	
1729	Jane Bayly	Spinning	Henry Forrest	
1731	Mary Gibson	Spinster	William Clark	
1731	Thomas Gibson	Shepherd	Richard Coe	
1731	Augustus Handley	Husbandry	Eleanor and Francis Dadsley	
1731	William Gibson	Husbandry	John Porter	
1731	John Gibson	Husbandry	John Flower	
1734	Anne Gibson	Spinster	Mark Sansam	Yeoman
1734	William Bayly	Husbandry	Walter Brown	
1741	Francis Warrin	Husbandry	William Danson	
1741	Sarah Dewey	Spinster	William Hallister	
1741	Richard Trolley	Husbandry	Mary Wright	
1741	Francis Trolley	Spinster	John Jarvis	
1742	Nichol Warren	Husbandry	William Dadsley	
1742	John Warren	Husbandry	Joseph Dikes	
1743	John Littledyke	Husbandry	John Brewitt	
1749	Sarah Parnham	Spinster	Francis Vincent	

Clearly the parish was passing to local men the responsibility for rearing orphans and teaching them a trade. The girls were to be taught housewifery, sewing, spinning and knitting, thus indicating a strong domestic industry derived from the sheep farming. The boys were to be taught the basic skills of husbandry or farming.

It is clear that the principal occupations came from farming. There is just the slightest hint that some framework knitting went on, in spite of the Manners' family attitude. In 1733 Thomas Greenfield, a framework knitter, was given a certificate acknowledging his Bottesford residence.

Even in 1812 there is evidence of a framework knitter in Bottesford. Blackner's 1815 *History of Nottingham* mentions that, of the 11,183 frames in Leicestershire, there were some in Bottesford. George Lamb, who died tragically in 1813, was 'a well known weaver and parish sexton. He had, however, fallen out with a neighbour and in a fit of temper had told the man that he would cut his throat under his window and haunt him for the rest of his life'. Perhaps he was the last of the Bottesford men who earnt their living from textile crafts. By the 19th century there were no full scale textile crafts in the village.

The male-oriented nature of early records tends to mask the number of working women. The Duke of Rutland seemed happy to tolerate, indeed to encourage great numbers of women working at home. By 1851, 35 women were employed as lace runners. This nineteenth century craft followed the invention of lace-making machines. These were first invented in Nottingham by John Leavers around 1813. As lace historians Lowe and Richards point out, 'it was never Leavers' intention to make fancy lace, because at this time machine made lace net was mostly marketed plain, with elementary motifs such as spots or sprigs and the finer ornamentation put in by hand by the lace runner'. The lace runners ran the home, helped on the smallholding, made butter, cheese and clothes and in their spare time stitched beautiful patterns on machine lace for the lace-mad Victorian middle-class. Some Bottesford lace runners were recorded in the 1851 census: Sarah Hallam, Sarah Branstone, Catherine Stray, Ann Bust, Hannah Bust, Ann Harvey, Mary Smith, Ann Smith, Elizabeth Haynes, Elizabeth Rawden, Elizabeth Parnham, Elizabeth Hickson, Ann Knowles, Mary Challands, Sarah Brown, Mary Bent, Ann Hardy, Bridget Hallam, Elizabeth Barratt, Elizabeth Gilding, Sarah Gilding, (aged 12), Mary Adams, Sarah Wells, Ann Deacon, Mary Bust, Ann Bust, Sarah Hollingworth, Ann Dent, Ann Johnson, Ann Parnham and Mary King. Thomas Goodson, son of Isabelle Goodson who farmed Muston Gorse Farm for the Duke, was described in 1851 as a lace manufacturer. Otherwise all occupations were derived from the soil.

One family with a craft of major significance were the Challands, an old Bottesford family first recorded locally in 1572. They were well established as freeholders, voting in the 1830 parliamentary election. Joseph was a brickmaker and bricklayer and William, his son, a carpenter. Such builders created the lovely red brick houses of Bottesford. Joseph Walker was the tile maker for Challands and John Gibson was a brickmaker. By 1851 there were 27 men earning their living from brickmaking or bricklaying, building houses for a rapidly growing population.

Carpentry was an associated trade; James Lewty's son, William, was apprenticed to a joiner in 1851. The Lewty family, James Spencer and his wife, Jane, their son, James, and his wife, Fanny, lived opposite the Cross and Stocks. Their trade of watch and clockmaker has spread the name of Bottesford across the East Midlands and today their clocks fetch over £1,000! But there were few such skilled craftsmen: most men and women with these important carpentry skills were involved in house building, furniture and farm implement repair and the vital trade of coffin making. At Lady Adeliza Norman's funeral 'the order for the coffin was entrusted to the firm of Mrs Hannah Norris, carpenter etc and was executed in a thoroughly workmanlike manner by her employees. It would be difficult to imagine anything more beautiful than the grain of the oak brought out by elaborate polishing' reported the *Grantham Journal*. In 1851 there were four master carpenters in the village.

A trade even more closely related to agriculture was milling. The early concentration on grain brought about several water mills by 1086. There were still two water mills at Bottesford in the 17th century – Easthorpe, which survived as a working mill into the 20th century, and one 50 yards upriver from the churchyard. By 1702 the latter, on the Dorking Poor Farm, was ruinous. The Trustees apparently decided to 'let it fall' and reduced the farm tenant, Mrs Elizabeth Cain's rent, by £8 over two years. They received 5s 'in earnest for the mill' ruins. Mill technology was improving, less grain was being produced and so the Dorking Poor water mill disappeared – today there is no trace of it at all. The Sedgebrook water mill, used by Muston folk since the time of the Colvilles, was finally dismantled in the 1960s. Mr Brian Slater preserved the millstones.

It is the same story with windmills. There were four in Bottesford – one on Beacon Hill, one in Queen Street, one on the west side of Belvoir Road, which was called Mill Lane earlier this century, and the fourth at the Canal. All traces of machinery and towers have disappeared. The Normanton Mill is recorded on 18th century maps, in addition to Easthorpe and Sedgebrook water mills. When the Grantham Canal was constructed in the 1790s, a mill was built alongside the canal, to grind corn which could then easily be transported to Grantham or Nottingham. During the 19th century two further windmills were built, one closer to the village and one, in Queen Street, with steam power to supplement the capricious wind.

But it was Easthorpe Water Mill which proved the longest-lasting and the most remunerative. In 1851 Trophimus Lane worked the Mill with three men and three boys, assisted by his brother, Marshall Lane, at 27 already a retired police officer. William Barnsdale worked the Belvoir Road Mill on the edge of the 19th century village: he employed two men. The Top Mill on the canal was worked by Thomas Whittle. By 1857 the Normanton Mill appears to have stopped working and the Top Mill and Barnsdale's Mill are both referred to as the 'two Wind Corn Mills'. John Longbottom worked the Queen Street Mill in 1851. It is probable that Thomas Scrimshaw worked the Muston Mill in 1830 and this water mill on the boundary between Muston and Sedgebrook was called alternatively Sedgebrook or Muston. Later he worked the Top Mill, which became known as Scrimshaw's Mill. Though the water mills outlasted the windmills, the 18th century and 19th century preference was for windmills explained by William Pitt in 1805: 'water mills were a great hindrance to the extension and adoption of water meadows as the millers traditionally imposed their demands for water above all others'. The mills ground corn and rolled oats, producing malt for locally brewed beer and grinding maize for the Belvoir estate pheasants. The Easthorpe Mill machinery was actually worked from 1853 for a century by one family, the Baines; they could produce a tone of bread flour a day and they also ground meal for the Castle pigs.

Another trade with a remarkable topographical stability was butchery. Two butchers, John Aenycourt and George Gardener, were listed in the 1381 Bottesford Poll Tax return; they were also two out of only four recorded in the Leicestershire Vale of Belvoir villages. As grazing developed so several graziers killed their own beasts; Daniel Daybell of the Dorking Poor Farm was listed as a butcher in 1846. The two other butchers in the village that year were William Jackson and John Riley. By 1851 William Jackson was in High Street next to the premises used by Eric George in the late 20th century. He had one apprentice, William Bradley. James Riley was a Master Butcher, by the Cross, the predecessor of Taylors today. The third butcher, J.D. Robinson, developed a pork pie speciality towards the end of the 19th century, and his shop was eventually in Market Street, the premises of the third modern butcher, Goodsons.

There was something of a scramble for business by the butchers and the bakers over the famous local pork pies. J.D. Robinson sold his pies to Royalty, aristocracy and the gentry – although Royalty was really Miss Harriet Winn, the daughter of a local smallholder who, in the 1890s, went into service at Buckingham Palace, where she worked for 40 years. One of J.D. Robinson's rivals was pork pie king, and Chapel Street baker, Mr Lane. There were generally two or three master bakers; two were listed in 1851: John Hardy on High Street and William Page in Chapel Street. To complement the pies David Hoe set up a sauce works near the Easthorpe Mill. He produced Belvoir and Bengal Chutneys patronized by the Prince of Wales, the Duke of Rutland and members of the Melton Hunt.

Most people in the village up to 1850 were virtually self-sufficient, buying some groceries but brewing their own beer and baking if they had an oven. They bought straw bonnets from the many straw bonnet makers, of whom there were five in 1851. It was in that year, though, that Bottesford was to be irrevocably changed by the opening of the railway. Many jobs became available and the railway and train service for the first time made it possible to live there and work somewhere else.

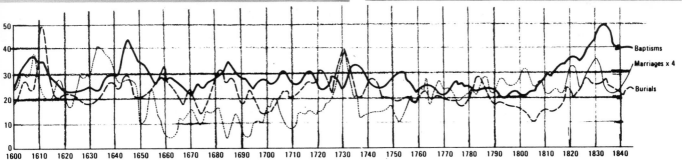

LEFT: Stenwith windmill, close to Muston. (LCC) RIGHT: Site of Queen Street Mill. (HER) BELOW: Population statistics 1600-1840 for Bottesford. (DL)

51

LEFT: A 17th century shoe found in the village. These were hidden away in cupboards to ward off evil. (SM) ABOVE: Letter posted to Muston in the 1740s. BELOW: The post office, on the right, in the 1920s. (PM) RIGHT: Mr Harold Brewster. (DB) OPPOSITE ABOVE: Mr Nelson Parnham — postman in the 1980s. (BH) RIGHT: Mr George's shop in 1910, next to a building which is Doctor Glencross's surgery in 1989. (HER) CENTRE: High Street today — Mr Eric George's butcher's shop next to the Post Office. BELOW LEFT: Mr Eric George in 1989. RIGHT: Mr Charles Brewster, butcher for Goodson's in 1989.

ABOVE: Mr Robert Taylor, outside his slaughterhouse in 1989. LEFT: Mr John Taylor, butcher for Taylor's in 1989. (BH) RIGHT: One of James Lewty's clocks. (RC)

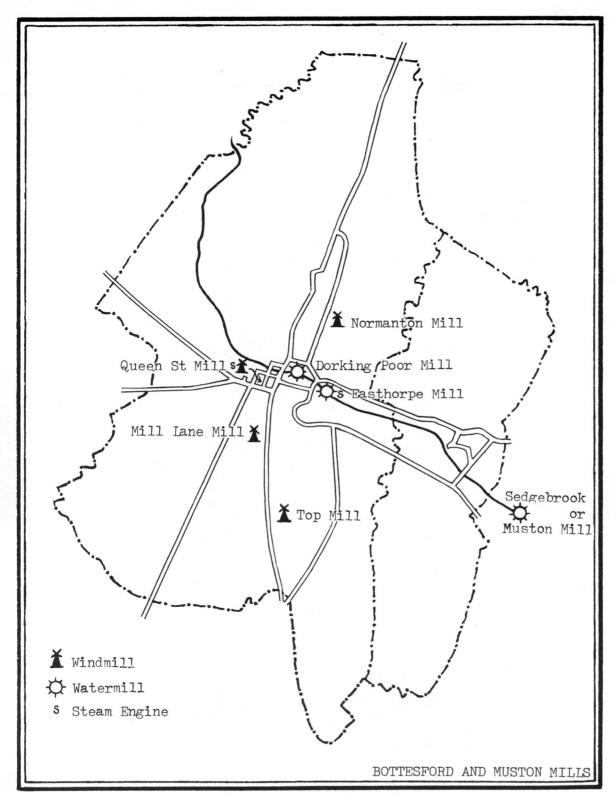

Normanton Mill

Queen St Mills

Dorking Poor Mill

s Easthorpe Mill

Mill Lane Mill

Top Mill

Sedgebrook
or
Muston Mill

Windmill

Watermill

s Steam Engine

BOTTESFORD AND MUSTON MILLS

Bottesford and Muston Mills.

ABOVE: Fleming's Bridge — from the east, (DB) and LEFT: from the west. (VPE) RIGHT: The bridge over the ford leading to the Green. BELOW: The Devon in the village.

Road versus Rail

In 1850 the railways came. They brought access to Grantham, Nottingham and all stations beyond. In 1851 ten Bottesford men were employed on the railway and this was increased to 17 by 1871. The ironstone line brought minerals to the extensive Bottesford sidings from the workings behind Belvoir Castle. By the beginning of the 20th century the railway had become a commuter line, with many men going to Hornsby's ironworks in Grantham. Perhaps the most vital link the railway provided was for farmers, for contracts with United Dairies in London and the Co-op in Nottingham offered regular income, provided the churns of milk from the Lincoln Reds and the Shorthorns were ready on time. Millers used the line to market their flour; there were excursion trains, taking Bottesford people to the seaside and East Midland people in general for a short break in the Vale of Belvoir.

The railway companies seriously affected earlier forms of transport. Both the roads and canal suffered but, at the high point of village prosperity around 1870 and 1880, it was the roads which suffered most. There had been an extensive road system in and around Bottesford for centuries. The earliest roads were prehistoric tracks associated with Sewstern Lane, east of the parish. It is almost certain that a branch left Sewstern Lane going north-west to Hazelford Ferry on the Trent, passing through Bottesford. This road can be followed along much of its route; it becomes a green lane in Flintham parish. But the railway line of the 1880s, the Great Northern, and London and North Western Joint Railway (GN & LNWJR) destroyed the track completely, although earlier enclosure had probably ended its serious use as a road. Again, there were innumerable paths in earlier days of which there are traces in the charters. The road to the Castle was Kastelgate in the 13th century. There was a road called le Grene at the same time: this perhaps is the green lane mentioned in 1350 and 1398, probably Long Hedge Lane. The road to Orston was Tawstongate; another road in the 14th and 15th centuries was Prestegate and both Prestegate and Castelgate are mentioned again in a 1493 document. There are many tantalizing references in early documents to main roads, *eg* a 13th century reference to the Newerc Road in the south of the parish. Stodgate probably meant the road leading to Stodam's Fee, land in the south of the parish. The widespread feature of crosses on major roads is well documented in the 13th century, from the Cross 'standing in the road towards Redmile, up to the stone sited near Belvoir Priory and by the same stone up to the road of Belvoir towards Muston'. It is certain from these charters that the King's Highway passed through Bottesford. This was almost certainly a north-south road, for an outlaw, banished from the land in 1426, was to be conducted by the constable of Bottesford to Belvoir by the King's Road.

This King's Highway was probably the Newark Road and it would have passed through Bottesford, close to the Market Cross. The Cross is generally dated to the end of the 14th century, erected by the de Roos family both as a site for both a market and for preaching. There is no trace of a charter for this market, but it is safe to assume from the Cross the existence of a regular market on its site. This suggests an east-west road at the junction there with the

King's Highway. There were pathways to all the neighbouring villages, including one only recently lost, from the southern end of Normanton to Kilvington *via* Mary Bridge across the Devon. This path probably started in Normanton at the site of the chapel-of-ease in Normanton, for ruined stonework still survived in 1792. As Nichols put it 'The chapel is now down and scarcely a trace to be found, though walls were standing within the memory of man, but reserved for the use of barns, roads etc'. A similar chapel-of-ease possibly existed in Easthorpe although, unlike the Normanton chapel, there is no documentary evidence. Again its exact site is lost; it was probably at the junction of Muston Lane and Easthorpe Road, where possibly a cross once stood.

The east-west road from Grantham to Nottingham only gradually became the most significant road in the parish. This changing orientation, relating more to Grantham, Bingham and Nottingham than to Newark and Belvoir, developed during the 17th and 18th centuries, and eventually the Grantham/Nottingham road was turnpiked, beginning in 1758. This road was increasingly used by heavy carriages bringing coal, which increased in price enormously the further one was from the pits. There were probably two tollgates on the road in Bottesford: one immediately to the east of the junction of Orston Lane and the Nottingham Road, and one by the Cross and Stocks. A tollgate survived and is in the keeping of a branch of the Leicestershire Museum Service at Oakham. But the railway killed off the turnpike; the road was de-turnpiked on 1 November 1876 and grass grew in Bottesford High Street.

The main road along the High Street remained quiet and calm up to the First World War. Thereafter, the road became increasingly congested and the idea of a by-pass was mooted. In the October 1968 parish magazine, the *Cross and Stocks*, E.J. Cox said that the 'by-pass has been in the air for something like 30 years or more'. A correspondent in December 1968 asked if anyone did 'really think it will come to pass during the next twenty years'. Today that gives us a 50 year span for the by-pass campaign, from 1935 to the 1980s! The problem lay in two quite appalling bends: one at the Washdyke Bridge, which was ironed out with a new bridge in 1936 (incidentally removing the sheep dip and its associated pinfold), and the other, the bend by the school. The obvious route to the north of the village, which would involve spoiling lower quality land, was effectively prevented by the railway line – skewed bridges would have been expensive. The final solution, a three mile road from Muston to Orston Grange, was eventually accepted: there had been 16 accidents on the High Street between 1984 and 1987, involving personal injury. The by-pass was finally planned and financed by the Government in the year of the 1987 general election. It was opened in March 1989 and proved a wonderful asset to the village, which overnight reverted to its pre-war calm. Old people ventured out who previously had been too worried by the lorries thundering through, and so there was an increase in shopkeepers' trade.

The minor roads have always been the responsibility of a local authority – the manor court, then the overseers of the highways of the Parish, and now a combination of Parish District and County Councils. In 1577 the manor court fined Thomas Dymock 4d for not clearing his dung heap off the highway before Pentecost. Thereafter, for three centuries, the Parish was responsible for its own minor roads and the normal practice was for the village poor to be employed on their upkeep. In 1834 the rates of pay for parish roadmen were laid down on 1 December 1831: 'none more than 12s' a week. A single man on the highway earned 3s a week, if married 5s, with one child 6s 3d, with two children 7s 6d, with three 8s 9d and with four 10s. The salary of the surveyor of the highways was £30 a year. The overseers of the poor in 1837 were George Whitehead and Joseph Challands. Joseph was among 21 village employers in 1837 who agreed to take labourers only from Bottesford, in order to protect local employment.

Village street names have changed frequently. Mill Lane was so named when it led to two mills – it has become Belvoir Road. Westhorpe has disappeared and by 1874 the usage was West End. In 1851 Chapel Street was so called after the Methodist Chapel of 1845 (with Wright's Yard leading off). Pinfold Lane was also called the Nook in the early 19th century, but it was called Pinfold Lane in 1894. Richards Court was a set of houses leading south from the High Street. In the 19th century the houses round the Cross had the address Near the Cross. Queen Street received its name after Queen Victoria by 1846 but there was no Albert Street then, for in 1851 it was Back Lane. The Green could be the oldest street name. Normanton has never had any street names. In Easthorpe the main street was Belvoir Road in 1851 – this is now Castle View Road. What is now Easthorpe Road was Poplar Street in 1851 – where are the poplars now? The road to the station was called Blue Bank and the Bunkers Hill Poor Houses were so called throughout the 19th century. It is strange to find that Church Street was regarded as in Easthorpe in 1851. The Wyggeston cottages were called Spalton's Row in 1851, after Olivia Spalton, the farmer who was the Wyggeston tenant. Rutland Lane, when it was the main road, was known as the Ramper or Rampart.

Few 'buses have travelled these streets; indeed the village 'bus service has never been particularly good. By 1851 the railway ensured fast and effective travel to and from Grantham, Bingham and Nottingham, which were becoming the main destinations of Bottesford workers and shoppers. A local 'bus service run by Randalls flourished after the Second World War. In the late 1980s there are three 'buses serving the village: one to Melton Mowbray eight times a day, a similar number go to Bingham and Newark, and three go daily to and from Grantham and Nottingham. There are no Sunday 'bus services.

This relatively limited 'bus service reflects the reliance on the railway which has been so vital a part of Bottesford since the 1850s. An example of this is the rather sad story of a day in the life of William Welbourn, the village schoolmaster. Richard Kettleborrow, the grazier who farmed at the Nook, was taken ill in September 1857. Mr Welbourn called on him 'this morning about 8 o'clock and found him insensible and very bad'. There was a problem over the will and Mr Manners, the Grantham lawyer, was expected that evening to execute a codicil. Dr Singleton was summoned to Mr Kettleborrow's bedside and declared 'his unfitness to sign any such document'. William Welbourn was in a quandary, so he took action: 'By the next train I went to Grantham and saw Mr Manners, reported the state of Mr Kettleborrow's health to him and his indisposing state of mind. Manners entrusted the codicil into my hands to be executed if any lucid interval should arise offering a proper opportunity so to do. On my return about 3 o'clock I found Mr Kettleborrow dead, a few minutes before. Consequently the codicil was never executed and the estate saved £300 – a very good job I think for the children'. The train service made such a return journey possible in a short time.

This was the Ambergate Railway, opened in July 1850. There were great celebrations in Grantham: the richer people dined on a 'sumptuous cold collation' and 'the other portion of the community were highly amused by Mr Wilson, landlord of the Blue Dog Inn, who got up a variety of rustic sports and where prizes were awarded to successful competitors, for hats, gowns, pieces, boots, ribbons, legs of mutton and various other minor articles'. From the time-table, William Welbourn could have caught the 10.10 from Nottingham, arriving in Bottesford at 10.58 getting to the Ambergate Station in Grantham at 11.15. He could then have caught the 2.20 from Grantham, returning to Bottesford for 2.38. The fastest train in July 1852 to London from Bottesford would have involved changing at Grantham and catching the 7.10, arriving at King's Cross at 11.00 – four hours to the Capital from Bottesford.

The line to Nottingham became important in the politics of railway companies, for the GNR were anxious to get access to the Nottinghamshire coal fields. In 1854 the Ambergate Railway was leased to the GNR for 999 years and the GNR constructed huge sorting yards at Colwick, Nottingham. As a result, Bottesford's mineral traffic developed and the village became a significant railway centre. The ironstone from the Belvoir ridge came onto the main line at the Belvoir Junction in Muston, which opened in 1883 and closed in 1976. Schoolboys going to Sedgebrook Grammar School used the line. Seaside excursions from Nottingham to Skegness increased the quantity of traffic along the main line.

For a few brief years Bottesford had two working stations: the main line station, and Bottesford South on the GN and L & NW Joint Railway, from Newark south to Melton and Market Harborough. The South Station was 'fairly large with a goods yard beyond the passenger station, the goods yard being on the up side of the line. On the down side there was another yard with access to the public road. The station master's house was on the up side'. The line was opened on 15 December 1879, and the first through trains were from Northampton and Market Harborough to Newark, with four trains a day from January 1880 until 1883. Thereafter the Bottesford South Station was closed – lasting three years only. The line itself survived as there were spurs to the main GNR line, ideal for Leicester or Melton people to get to Grantham and the east coast. By the late 1930s there were five Grantham-Leicester trains *via* Bottesford each day. Why was this line built at all, when it proved so unsuccessful?

The problem originally was getting approval. The hunting lobby was concerned about a line through the hunting country of four hunts – the Belvoir, Quorn, Cottesmore and Fernie. But the discovery of ironstone in the area in the 1860s made the prospect of a link connecting with Newark and the GNR to the north seem profitable. Ironstone could go north to the industrial West Riding and Yorkshire wool could come south to the Leicestershire hosiery industry. But it proved a financial flop and was finally shut down in the 1970s. Thereafter there was no hope of reopening, as the Bottesford by-pass destroyed the permanent way south of Bottesford and used much of the hard core from the line to the north. It had proved of value during the Second World War, when petrol was brought to Bottesford and processed at the RASC camp; the line to Redmile gave access to storage tanks there. Today the railway has gone, leaving only the occasional bridge for the railway enthusiast to wonder over, like the Three Arch Bridge, just north of the village.

The railways and the roads were developed through Bottesford as a result of mineral interests, first coal, later ironstone. One further transport system was developed which linked the agricultural pre-occupation of the village with the new interest in coal – this was the Grantham Canal. For over 50 years after 1800, villagers' coal was delivered from the Grantham Canal. It was brought to local farms and houses in the 1840s by two coal dealers, William Piggins and Olivia Spalton. The Canal was constructed largely with Nottingham money, but there were several local shareholders. Richard Bartram bought three £100 shares, and Rev John Thoroton, the Rector of Bottesford, bought two. John Hand, the sheep breeder, bought two, William King, the Duke's agent and the engineer responsible for the eastern section of the canal, 10 shares, investing £1,000 in his own enterprise. The 5th Duke was a minor at the time; five £100 shares were bought for him. For many years a steady return on capital was the reward – sometimes as high as 13% per annum. One use of the Canal was the transport of corn and coal; but perhaps the most significant use in the long run was the enormous quantities of building material and fertiliser. It was realised from 1799, when the Canal really got into its stride, that 'the lime trade will be very considerable for in no county is it more necessary than on the clays near the line'. Dung, night soil, marl and ashes went toll-free at the Trent Lock, and contributed enormously to the agricultural prosperity of the Parish in the first half of the 19th century. It also helped with the great rebuilding in the 1830s and 1840s. In December 1854 the Canal Company was bought out by the Ambergate Railway, and it slowly declined until it was shut to through traffic in 1935. Although the Canal brought a measure of prosperity to the parish, it was undoubtedly the railway which opened it up. It was said at the opening of the Ambergate line in 1850 that it 'cheapened the article of coal alone full 50% . . . corn merchants, millers and other dealers profited from the railway' and 'fat and lean stock will now be transmitted to different farms and markets in this and adjoining counties and artificial manures will be taken back at the trifling outlay'. Thus the *Stamford Mercury* eulogised the new railway, which opened up life for the village in an unprecedented way.

ABOVE LEFT: The footbridge by the ford. (HER) RIGHT: The Washdyke Bridge with Bunker's Hill in the background, (DB) and BELOW LEFT: the modern road bridge which has replaced it. (HER) RIGHT: Granary Lane. (HER)

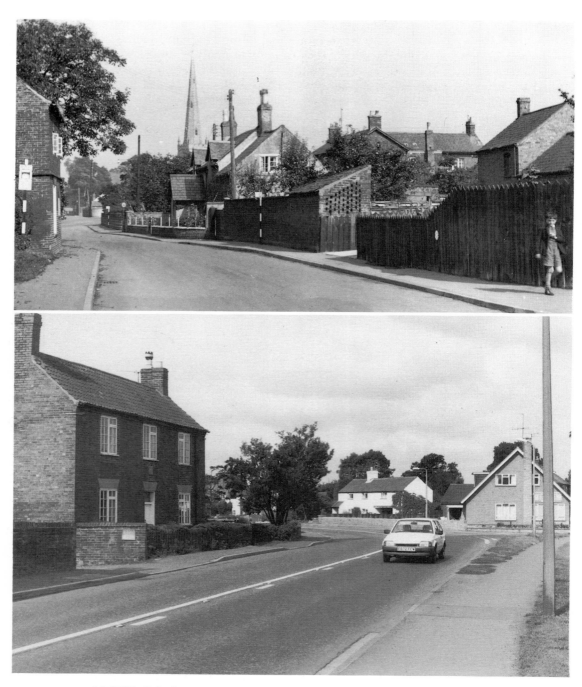

ABOVE: Belvoir Road and Market Place, Bottesford, 1930s. BELOW: The site of the Toll Bar in High Street — the house on the left was built for John Brewitt. (PM)

ABOVE: The Grantham Road petrol station locally built in the 1950s
(WJR) and BELOW: in 1989. CENTRE: The by-pass under
construction in 1988. (HER)

63

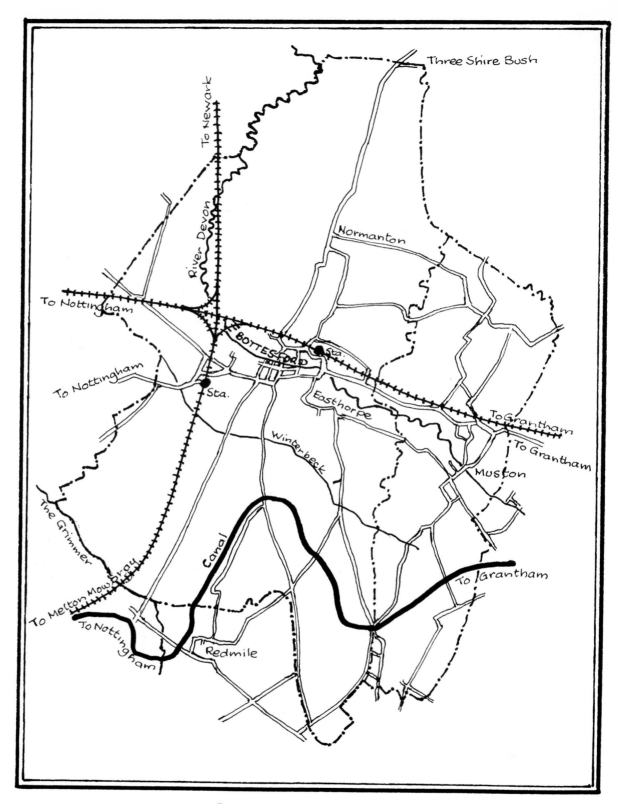

Roads, canal and railways. (VPE)

64

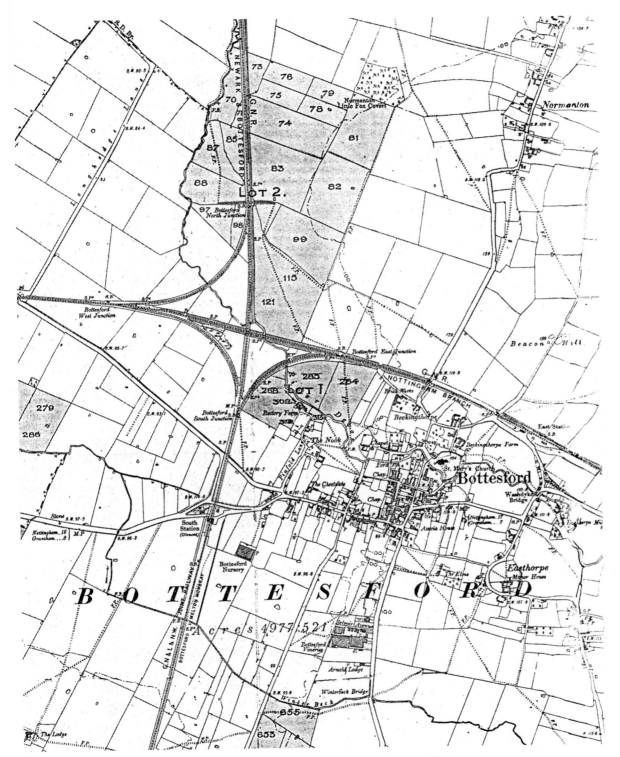

The village in 1920, showing footpaths and railways.

ABOVE: The disused South Station, BELOW: The village station today.
OPPOSITE: Timetable of the Northampton-Newark trains on the GN
and LNWJR — 1886.

August 1887
Market Harborough, Leicester, Nottingham, Grantham & Newark. Great Northern and London & North Western Joint Railway

	a.m	a.m	a.m	a.m	a.m	a.m	a.m	a.m	a.m	p.m	a.m	p.m	p.m	p.m	p.m	p.m		SUN. a.m
Euston dep.		5.15			7.30		9.30			11.0	1.30		3.0			4.30		
Oxford dep.						9.00			9.50	12.5		2.30			3.30			
Northampton		7.00		9.15		11.0			12.45	3.0		4.40			6.0			
Market Harbro'		7.47		10.10		11.30			1.45	3.45		5.22			6.30			
Hallaton		7.59		10.22					1.57	3.57		5.34			1			
East Norton		8.4		10.27					2.2	4.3		5.40			1			
Tilton		8.12		10.34					2.9	4.11		5.48			1			
Leicester dep.	7.23		8.20	9.5		10.25	11.45	12.40				4.8			6.25			8.30
Humberstone	7.27		8.24	9.9		10.30		12.44				e			6.29			8.35
Thurnby	7.33			9.15		10.36		12.50							6.35			8.41
Ingersby xx	7.39			9.21		10.42		12.56				4.20			6.41			8.48
Loseby	7.45			9.27		10.48		1.2							6.47			8.55
John O'Gaunt	7.50	8.20	8.41	9.32	10.41	10.53		1.7	2.16	4.18	4.30	5.55	6.52	7.1			9.1
Great Dalby	7.56	8.27			10.47			1.12	2.22	4.25		L	6.58	L			
Melton arr.	8.2	8.34	8.51	9.42	10.53	11.5	12.4	12.14	1.19 2.28	4.32	4.40	6.6	7.4	7.11			9.11
Mowbray dep.	7.40 8.3	8.36	8.52	9.43	10.55	11.6	12.6	12.15	1.20 2.29	4.47	4.41	Stop	7.5	7.12			9.12
Scalford	7.51 8.9	8.42		9.49	11.1	11.12			1.26 2.35	4.53			7.13				
Long Clawson and Hose	8.1 8.16	8.46		9.53	11.5	11.15			2.40	4.58			7.18 7.20				
Harby * arr.	8.9 8.19	8.52		9.59	11.11	11.22	12.18	12.27	1.34 2.45	5.4	4.53		7.18 7.20				
Harby * dep.	8.15	8.53			11.13	12.21			2.46	5.5			7.31				
Barnston	8.29	9.1			11.20				2.54	5.13			7.39				
Bingham Road	8.41	9.9			11.27				3.1	5.20			7.46				
Radcliffe arr.	8.49	9.17			11.34				3.8	5.27			7.53				
Radcliffe dep.	8.52	9.18			11.35				3.9	5.28			7.54				
Netherfield +	9.1	9.25			11.41	12.38			3.15	5.34			8.0				
Nottingham arr.	9.10	9.31			11.47	12.46			3.21	5.40			8.6				
Harby * dep.		8.21		10.0		11.32			1.35			4.54	3.45	7.28				
Redmile x		8.27		9.10 10.6		11.38			1.41			5.0	3.50	7.34			9.30
Bottesford		8.35		924 n		11.45			1.48			n		d			9.39
Sedgebrook		8.43 g			g	11.52			sig.								
Grantham arr.		8.51 10.13		10.23 12.44		12.0			2.0 3g52 7g5			5.15	4.7	7.50			
Harby * dep.						11.23	12.31										
Redmile x						11.29	12.37										
Cotham						11.41											
Newark arr.						11.50	12.55			5b43							

August 1887
Newark, Grantham, Nottingham, Leicester & Market Harborough. Great Northern and London & North Western Railway

	a.m	a.m	a.m	a.m	p.m	p.m	p.m	p.m	p.m	p.m	p.m	p.m	p.m		SUN. p.m
Newark dep.	5b21		8b59	9b47	1.48		3.10		6.0						
Cotham							sig.		sig.						
Redmile x					2.7		3.29		6.19						
Harby * arr.					2.13		3.35		6.25						
Grantham dep.	7.37		9.25	9g55	10.55 12.15		3.0	5.30				7.57			7.53
Sedgebrook	a		sig.	a	12.22		j	k			8.8	8.5			7.59
Bottesford	749		a	a	12.29		a	k			8.14	8.12			
Redmile x	7.56		9.43	11.13 12.35			3.19	5.51				8.18			
Harby * arr.	8.1		9.49	11.18 12.40			3.25					8.23			
Nottingham dp.		8.0	9.20	10.40		1.53	3.5		6.5						
Netherfield +		8.6	9.26	10.46		1.58	3.11		6.11						
Radcliffe ar.		8.10		10.50		2.3									
" dep.		8.11	a	10.51		2.4	a								
Bingham Road		8.19		10.58		2.11	3.24		6.22						
Barnston		8.26	m	11.5		2.18	3.31		6.30						
Harby * arr.		8.35	9.44	11.13		2.25	3.40		6.36						
" * dep.	8.2	8.37	9.51	11.20	11.25 12.41	2.28	3.42	5.57	6.26	6.37		8.24			
Long Clawson and Hose	8.8	8.44		c	11.31 h		3.51			6.43					8.10
Scalford	8.13	8.48		c	11.36 12.50					6.49					8.13
Melton arr.	8.19	8.55	10.4	11.35	11.42 12.56	2.39	3.57	6.9	6.38	6.55	8.36	8.41			
Mowbray dep.	8.20	8.57	10.5	11.37	11.44 12.57	2.40	3.58	6.15	6.40	6.56	7.3	8.37	8.43		8.28
Great Dalby	8.27	9.5		c	11.53 1.4		4.5	6.22			7.10		8.51		8.28
John O'Gaunt	8.33	9.13	10.17	11.50	11.58 1.9		4.12	6.29	6.52	7.8	7.17	8.52	8.58		8.34
Loseby	8.39				12.3 1.14						7.22		9.3		8.41
Ingersby xx	8.45				12.9 1.20						7.28		9.9		8.48
Thurnby	8.51				12.15 1.26						7.34		9.15		8.53
Humberstone	8.57				12.21 1.32				d		7.40	9.10	9.20		8.59
Leicester arr.	9.1				12.26 1.37				7.10		7.45	9.16	9.26		
Tilton		9.21	10.25	11.58			4.19	6.36							
East Norton		9.29		12.6			4.27	6.44							
Hallaton		9.35		12.12			4.33	6.50	sig.						
Market Harbro'		9.45	10.42	12.22		3.15	4.44	7.0	7.32						
Northampton		10.36	11.8	1.3		3.50	5.31	7.48	8.10						
Oxford arr.			2.55			6.2	7.21	10.21	10.21						
Euston arr.		12.36	1.0	2.55		5.40	7.20	10.15	10.15						

a Stops when required to take up. b via Grantham. c Stops when required to take up for Tilton and beyond. d Stops when required to set down. e Stops when required to take up for Grantham and stations north of Grantham. f Stops when required to set down. g via Radcliffe. h Stops to take up for Leicester line. j Stops on Weds. and on Tuesdays when required to set down. g via Radcliffe. h Stops to take up for Leicester line. m Stops on Sats. to set down from Sats. to take up for Long Clawson. k Stops on Sats. to take up for Melton and Leicester. m Stops on Sats. to set down from Nottingham. p Change for Leicester arr. 4.43. * Harby & Stathern. + Netherfield & Colwick. x Station for Belvoir. xx Station for Ingersby. sig. Train stops by signal to take up.

ABOVE: The Red Lion in the 19th century. (DB) CENTRE: The Wheatsheaf or the Gap — Muston. (HER) BELOW: The former Six Bells beerhouse, owned originally by the Wyggeston Hospital. (HER)

Bricks, Blessings and Bread

Transport by canal or rail solved a problem which bedevilled any village like Bottesford, which was some distance from a major river. Most village churches in the area were built of local ironstone and indeed the parish church of St John the Baptist, Muston, is mainly ironstone, with limestone cornerstones for strength. We simply do not know how the limestone used for St Mary's Bottesford was brought here. What we can appreciate is the intensity of religious feeling which led to so many religious foundations in the neighbourhood being built to the glory of the Blessed Virgin Mary, as were 13 of the Vale of Belvoir churches. Such was the depth of piety of English people that England was considered as 'our Lady's Dowry'. The Bottesford Parish Church was dedicated to 'Mary, the mother of Jesus'. A chantry dedicated to Mary was established within the Parish Church in the 14th century. Much earlier, by 1086, the Priory founded at the foot of the Castle was also dedicated to Mary. At Stathern a chantry dedicated to her was established.

The Parish Church today is a magnificent reminder of that intensely religious feeling of Bottesford people. It was built and rebuilt over 300 years – traces of Norman ironstone work survive in the chancel walls, from around 1150, and the final glory of the Church, the limestone tower and spire, date from the 14th and 15th centuries. Fuller in the 17th century described it as 'one of the primest churches, very fair and large with a high spire steeple'. Nichols was more ecstatic: 'one of the most beautiful ornaments of the Vale of Belvoir'. The pleasant name of The Lady of the Vale properly indicates the love Bottesford people have always felt for their glorious church.

St John's Church, Muston did not have the wealth of the de Roos family lavished on it as did St Mary's. The Church there was under the patronage of the prioress of Stixwold Convent in Lincolnshire and, as Nichols wrote: 'it is delightfully situated on the slope of a hill, under which the River Devon very beautifully meanders'. The living eventually passed to the Manners family, and they used their patronage wisely. In 1633 the 7th Earl, a man of independent opinion, appointed Robert Sanderson Rector of Muston. Sanderson was perhaps the greatest Anglican preacher of his generation; he was the Regius Professor of Divinity at Oxford, eventually becoming the reconciling and venerated Bishop of Lincoln in 1660. Henry Knewstub married Sanderson's grand-daughter, and was Rector of Muston for 40 years from 1665 to 1705. Fragments of his diary were published in 1792 by Nichols, ranging from the sublime to the ridiculous: '1670 May 16: At Belvoir, discoursed with Lord concerning transubstantiation' and 1669 July 26 'At Belvoir, coming home, *e lapsu equi os brachii fregi*, (broke my arm when my horse fell) and 1669 July 2 'By a fall from the house of office received a wound in my head. A strange accident: Lord bless me!' The other renowned Rector of Muston was George Crabbe, the outstanding poet and naturalist, whose account of the flora and fauna of the Vale of Belvoir was published by Nichols in Vol 1 of his *History of Leicestershire*. He was properly appreciative of the Manners family influence, writing in *The Village*

'In future times, when smit with Glory's charms,
The untried youth, first quits a father's arms –
Like MANNERS walk, who walk'd in Honour's way;
In danger foremost, yet in death sedate
Oh! be like him in all things but his fate!'

Crabbe suffered terribly while at Muston, for he was beset by nonconformist dissenters; he did not always reside in his rectory house and so the Methodists took advantage. They built a chapel, opened by John Hickman in 1802, much to Crabbe's annoyance. Non-conformist feeling in the area has always been strong, and Crabbe could not stop its development.

Bottesford has had four non-conformist chapels, a further testimony to the independence of local people. Non-conformity was not encouraged by the Lords of Belvoir, but a strong strain of Roman Catholicism has survived in the Manners family, which included several early 17th century adherents to the old faith. The first trace of Protestant non-conformity in Bottesford was in the 1780s, when a small society of Methodists met in the village, deriving strength from the Muston Methodists. The Bottesford Methodists became stronger and established their own chapel, built in 1820, from which they evangelised the Vale and Grantham. These Primitive Methodists belonged to that branch of dissent which believed in free will rather than strict predestination. This latter belief, that only the elect had access to grace, was held by Baptists who were also strong in the village.

The Particular Baptists built their chapel in 1789: there is a strong tradition of Baptist meetings in the Vale. The independence of local farmers and farm workers led to a strong Independent chapel in Melton Mowbray and a long-lived Independent chapel off Albert Street in Bottesford. In 1829 in Bottesford the three chapels had 86 members: 45 Primitive Methodists, 21 Particular Baptists and 20 Independents. In the 1851 census there were Baptist chapels in Bottesford, Hose, Long Clawson and Knipton; Wesleyan Methodist chapels in Bottesford, Plungar, Stathern, Harby, Hose, Long Clawson and Eaton; Primitive Methodist chapels in Bottesford, Redmile, Barklestone and Eaton. In Bottesford the Wesleyan Methodists built their chapel in 1845 and it became part of the Grantham circuit. When Methodism reunited (after the Second World War in this area) the Chapel Street building was sold off and Methodism concentrated in the original chapel off the Green. Mr W.J. Roberts converted the 1845 Chapel Street chapel into two houses and the 1820 chapel is being extended in 1989 to double its previous size. The Independent or Salem chapel, as it was sometimes known, struggled on through the 19th century, but was never as flourishing as the Methodists. In 1924 the building was sold by Mr George Norris   and it consisted of a 'ground floor · which was formerly used as a stable, open cow shed and trap house, and the upper floor which was formerly used as a chapel'. (In this house in the 1920s Miss Hester Tuxford wrote her *Cookery for the Middle Classes*, which went to eight editions).

Two chantries had been established in the middle of the 14th century in the Parish Church. Land was given to endow these charities, so that income should go to the maintenance of the two chantry priests, some of whose names have survived. The chaplain of the chantry of Our Lady in 1535 was Richard Brown, and Robert Peerson was the chaplain of the chantry of St Peter. The land consisted of a 'capital messuage near the rectory house with the land thereunto belonging lying in Normanton and Bottesford'. This land plus two cottages eventually came into the hands of Samuel Fleming, the Rector at the end of the 16th century, after the chantries had been dissolved by order of Henry VIII. The two cottages were turned into Samuel Fleming's Almshouses or Hospital for four aged widows of Bottesford. In 1835 the hospital contained six bedrooms, one sitting room and a kitchen, besides offices (toilets). The land provided income for the Almshouses and, at some stage around 1600, a barn or house was built 'not a great way from the centre of the town or the cross'. The Manse at the corner of Chapel

Street and Market Street was also on the Women's Hospital land. This became the curate's house and Rev Mr Clifton 'laid out a considerable sum in repairs in the 1820s'. The Rector's curates lived there until the First World War.

The Rector, or Parson as he was called, lived in the 'parsonage-house, a venerable old building', wrote Nichols in 1792. In the hall were long arched windows and a curious wooden roof, supported by two octagonal oak pillars. In it was a large staircase and gallery, railed by Dr Thomas White, who was rector here from 1679–1688. According to Mr Peck, a Stamford antiquary writing in the 1730s, 'Mr Ligonier, who left behind him a much respected name among the poor, repaired and beautified the parsonage house in 1702 and in particular new-floored the hall and built the fine staircase there'. This is the section of the Old Rectory still standing, described in 1788 as 'a parlour, study, kitchen, three chambers and three garrets mostly of stone and slated'. The oldest section of the building was pulled down by Rev Sir John Thoroton in 1789. Sir John was a keen architect, responsible for the rebuilding of Belvoir Castle after 1815, and he substantially rebuilt the Rectory. Considerable alterations happened between 1789 and 1985, when the buildings was sold by the Church Commissioners. The old tithe barn in 1788, 'thatched, part mud and stud, part brick and part stone', was removed after the Second World War along with extensive outbuildings. The main shell of Ligonier's building has now been beautifully restored by Mr K. Greasley and turned into attractive homes for retired people.

Mr Ligonier was a French Huguenot refugee who came to England c1680. He was recommended to the Countess of Rutland in 1687 by the Bishop of London as 'a very fit person to be with your sons. He has the character of a very honest man and a good scholar. He came here as a refugee, is well born and in every way qualified for such employment. I told him your salary was £40 yearly and he waits your orders'. He did well: he was eventually given the valuable living of Bottesford after being Vicar at Croxton Kerrial and Redmile. He was concerned about the schooling of the parish boys, which took place in the Church in a room adjoining the chancel. The Rector died in 1711 and devoted much of his will to establishing the Bottesford school. With help later from Anthony Ravell, the land which Ligonier gave proved adequate for the endowment of a proper school. In 1732 the Duke of Rutland had a new one built in the north-east corner of the churchyard, and the Ligonier/Ravell bequest provided an income for the schoolmaster, who had accommodation in the school. 28 children were to be educated freely 'to read the Bible, Prayers and Catechism of the Church of England'. It was at this school that D.R. Daybell learnt his letters and ciphering, enough to become a national figure in the late 19th century farming world. The school was pulled down in the 1850s and the Duke's foundation stone removed to the wall of the rectory, where it can still be seen. A new school was built opposite the Cross and Stocks in 1855, on the Duke's land and largely at his expense. This lasted over 100 years and is still considered a fine building. It has been replaced by two schools, one of which, Belvoir High School, was built by Mr W.J. Roberts, opening in 1958. The other is the attractive primary school, opened in 1977.

The Duke's family was also responsible for the other major almshouse in the village, the Earl of Rutland's Hospital, built in the 1590s. Documents survive relating to its construction, ordered by the Countess of Rutland in 1592 and fully endowed with extensive lands by the 5th Earl of Rutland in 1612. Elizabeth, the Countess of Rutland, no doubt intended the Hospital as a remembrance of her husband John, the 4th Earl, who died in 1588. She was developing the family tradition which held it essential to leave tangible memorials to the dead Earls. The Earls' famous tombs in the Church were started in the 16th century. Thomas, the first Earl, was buried with great ceremony; the plumber was paid 4s 4d for 'putting the corps in lead' and the alabaster man was paid £33 5s 8d' for making a tombe of alabastre for my lorde and my ladye, to be set at Botelford'. The Countess Elizabeth had to build two memorial tombs, for her husband John, the 4th Earl, had only survived his brother Edward, the 3rd Earl, for a year. On 16 October 1591 she paid 'two hunderithe pounds for the making of tolmes and settinge the same up at Bottesford for the towe lat Erles, Lord Edward and Lord John'. These memorials were constructed in London, sent by sea to Boston, and by cart to Bottesford. The journey was not easy and the agent of the Countess, Thomas Fairebarne, had to pay 8d for 'levers and roulls, and for a pece of woode to understoure the carte, which brake the axeltrie and stayed by the waye at Heather'. Six shillings were paid for 'foure hundereth breake [bricks] for the tomb'. William Hough, baker of Bottesford, was paid 10s 8d for suppers and breakfast for 17 persons coming with the 15 carriages from Boston to Bottesford.

Having set up the two tombs in 1591, the Countess Elizabeth now set about the building of the Almshouse. Her son Roger, now 5th Earl, was up at Cambridge. She ran the estate, controlling the tenancies, granting for £2 6s 8d a licence on 10 March 1591 to 'John Spreckley to marrye widowe Man, late wyfe to Roberte Man of Waltham, and to be admitted tenante to her ferme'. She had paid 'John Mathewe of Nottingham, painter in full payment of twentye pounde for inrichinge the towe tombes in Bottesforthe'. Then her agent, Richard Collyshawe, set about paying the accounts 'to builde the hospitall at Bottesforthe'. On 6 April 1592, Thomas Yernwoode of Stathorne, mason and slater, was paid £28 for 'buildinge the hospitall with mason worke'. Harry Scoffield of Wollisthorpe was paid 6s 6d for 'felling of ten oxes [oak trees] at Croxton for to builde the hospitall at Boltesforthe'. And most interesting to students of building: 'Paid, the XIth of June 1592, to Gregorye Porter, of Ancaster, in earneste, for xvi tune of freystone for the windows of the hospital at Bottesforthe, iiiid'. This means he was paid 4d for drawing up the contract to supply the Ancaster freestone, fine, grained limestone that could easily cut. We do not know the price of the stone, unfortunately. The hospital was apparently be finished by 1593, for in that year John Ley of Wollsthorpe, weaver, was paid 1½d a yard for 44 yards of cloth to make blankets for beds there and Elizabeth Preston and seven other women were paid 3d a day for '42 days at spininge and cardinge wolle for to make blankettes for the hospital'; 24 lbs of linen yarn were purchased from Gainsborough for counterpanes. Agnes Stevenson, Elizabeth Preston and Alice Shaw were paid 3d a day for 'dressinge, swinglinge and heckling flaxe for to make sheets and coverledges for the hospital'. This process was complex – it involved using a wooden instrument like a sword to beat and scrape flax so as to cleanse it of woody or coarse particles.

The Countess Elizabeth's son was Roger, the 5th Earl, who was deeply involved in the Earl of Essex's conspiracy in 1601 against Elizabeth I, and who spent some time in the Tower of London as a result. When he died in 1612 he directed that his brother, the 6th Earl, should 'finish a hospital in Bottesford (theretofore begun by his mother Elizabeth, Countess of Rutland) for six poor persons'. All the Earl's freehold lands in Muston were used for the endowment of the almshouses, hence the name of the Hospital Farm in Muston. Successive Earls and Dukes of Rutland added land, so that by 1819 the Men's Hospital estate consisted of 419 acres in Muston, Bottesford, Ab Kettleby and Long Clawson. In 1786 the stone hospital was extended in brick. According to a deed of 1762, 14 poor men resided there, being paid 10s 8d monthly with extensive perquisites. They were paid 6d at Easter, Whitsuntide, Bottesford Feast and Christmas for fire money, 10d in December in lieu of capon money, 6d in February and in August for salt, 10d in September for candles and 30s in April for a suit of clothes. Provision was made for each to have a good cloth gown every other Easter, 20 cwts of hard coals to be laid in May, and to provide bed and bedding, household goods, and all necessary utensils for their use and physic and attendance for such as should be sick; to pay 6s 8d at Ladyday and Michaelmas to a laundress for washing for each poor man'. Today the Hospital flourishes. Men and women live there in specially adapted flats. They no longer wear the uniform: 'blue gown, lined and turned up with white; and on the left shoulder is affixed an elegant silver badge on which appears a dual coronet of a peacock in pride within a garter'. By this Hospital the Manners family have carried out most effectively the wishes of Elizabeth, Countess of Rutland, nearly 400 years ago.

It was her other son, Francis, the sixth Earl of Rutland, who suffered from witchcraft. He had two sons and a daughter, all of whom suffered from illness which the doctors could not diagnose. When his oldest son died, it was suggested that such a tragedy could only be caused by the devil, working through witches. Three local women were arrested six years after the child's death and accused 'of wicked practice and sorcery'. The mother, Joan Flower, died, protesting her innocence, but her two daughters, Margaret and Philippa Flower, were hanged at Lincoln Castle in 1619. It is difficult today to understand such barbarity, but it arose from the overwhelming desire of the Manners family and the Bottesford Rector and people to find a scapegoat to explain the tragic loss of the Earl's son.

The Belvoir Castle family were responsible for helping to build housing for poorer Bottesford folk. There was a workhouse in the High Street during the 18th century, built on land given by the Dukes. The site of this is almost certainly now occupied by the bungalows built on the Hand's land. In 1891 George Hand, a descendant of John Hand, the ram breeder of Easthorpe Manor, conveyed the six cottages in the High Street, between John Sutton's land on the east and Henry George's land on the west, to a trust of seven Bottesford men (James and Frank Wright, surgeons, Francis Bartram, Richard Orton, Joseph Lenton, farmers, Arthur Hickson, miller and Robert Marriott, grocer and draper, and their heirs). The rents were to be used to keep up the property and pay £5 annually to the village school, and for 'purchasing food, fuel or clothing for the exclusive benefit of the deserving and needy poor of the Parish of Bottesford'. The cottages were all sold off and the present four bungalows built in 1962. The interest from the sale of the land still goes into a joint fund, made up from a range of charitable donations to the parish, and distributed annually.

The Duke also leased other land for cottages for the poor and in 1779 he had built a group of cottages on the land. The Parish then rented them at low rents. They were named to commemorate the opening battle in the American War of Independence, Bunker Hill. These cottages were all sold off in the 1920 Duke's sale. Their accommodation then varied from one living room and two bedrooms to three living rooms and three bedrooms. Each one had a coal hovel, a piggery and a good garden. These tiny cottages were commonplace throughout the village in the 18th and 19th centuries, generally in yards off the main roads. In 1851 there were eight of them in Richard Court, off the High Street, where agricultural labourers lived – George Richard was a lodging-housekeeper of High Street. In Wrights Yard, later called Redford's Yard, north of Chapel Street, there were eight houses with 46 people living in them. The Wyggeston Hospital owned some small cottages at the rear of the Six Bells. In 1851 the poor houses in Bunkers Hill held 17 families with 71 people. These figures give some indication of the great population explosion of the early 19th century, and the numbers cramped into old accommodation.

Once again the Duke came to the rescue of some Bottesford workers by building cottages for his tenants, notably the two pairs of brick and slated cottages in Easthorpe Road. He had always built good farms for his tenants, an excellent example being Beckingthorpe Farm. Church Farm was well looked after by the Dorking Poor. Perhaps the finest tenant farm is the Hospital Farm in Muston, a 16th century stone building. This is only rivalled by the Manor House in Easthorpe, to which it is possible to give a 15th century date as a result of the de Roos crest, so clearly carved and now set in the east wall.

The house in Easthorpe today called Bridge House was occupied in 1851 by a tenant of the Duke, Thomas Hoe: it was he, along with Joseph Challands, who made the bricks with which Bottesford was rebuilt in the 19th century. The Hoe brick yard was the other side of Easthorpe

Road from Bridge House, named after the Washdyke Bridge, where farmers brought their sheep to be washed. The other big brick yard in Beckingthorpe, developed by Joseph Challands, provided a large share of the thousands of beautiful bricks and tiles still so evident in the parish today. Some of the pantiles were a deep blue in colour, known today as the Bottesford Blues. A story still survives in the village that only one of Challands' tilemakers knew the secret of the glaze necessary to achieve the deep navy blue – and it died with him.

Some village houses still have traces of the original building material of earlier Bottesford housing – mud. The most complete example is 3 Castle View Road in Easthorpe, where there is now a brick first storey built onto a mud ground floor. In the garden there is a hovel (an all-purpose storage building) still with one wall of mud and an original wooden wall post – the rats have undermined the opposite wall, which is built in brick.

During the 20th century there has been an extraordinary explosion of building. Following the removal of many of the old cottages during the 1950s, when it was thought best to pull down 19th century houses, estates were built in the 1960s and 1970s to the east of Beckingthorpe and in the West End. Even more houses have been built in great numbers in the 1980s, so much so that, in place of the 350 buildings in Bottesford in 1894, there are now around 950 dwelling places in the confines of Bottesford village, 186 being built between 1981 and 1988. However, older buildings are now properly appreciated, and there are 32 listed buildings notified to the Melton Borough Council as being of special architectural or historic interest.

There are two listed bridges in the village – Fleming's Bridge built around 1600 with two ribbed segmental arches, and the late 18th or early 19th century small, redbrick bridge beside the Ford leading from Chapel Street to the Green. The three inns in the village are brick, the Red Lion and the Bull both being listed buildings from the 18th century or earlier. The Daybell Farm is a listed building now, as are the Nook farmhouse, the Rectory Farm and Church Farm. Indeed, Bottesford is so packed with listed buildings that several good ones, notably the Fleming almshouses of 1620 and earlier, have not yet achieved that status. There are 36 buildings notified to the Secretary of State for the Environment as being of local interest only. These include Acacia House, the Wyggeston Cottages, the Beckingthorpe Farm and the former National School opposite the Stocks and Cross.

Several official buildings are of interest, especially the attractive and listed police house of 1842. The railway station built in 1850 is now only a relic of its former self, as it has no staff at all. The station building was designed by T.C. Hine, the great Nottingham 19th century architect – his trademark of long, tall chimneys still survive. The original cast-iron lamp standard has been moved to the north-west side of the churchyard. There is no trace at all of what was popularly known as the smallest gasworks in the world – Bottesford had its own gasworks from 1866, but the northern industrial estate has now obliterated all sign of it. Finally, there still survive remnants of the Second World War in the Camp Farm industrial area on Orston Road and in the hangars from the airfield. Both of these structures were put up in 1940–41 and are now approaching 50 years old, something which was probably never dreamt of by the local and Irish labourers who put them up so long ago.

Rectors of Bottesford

–	Nicholas de Albinisco	1471	Thomas Burley	1679	Thomas White
1222	Ralph de Albinisco	1475	Mag. William Chauntre	1698	Abel Ligonier
1234	Nicholas de Belvero	1478 or 1479	Mag. Henry Bolem	1711	Lewis Griffin
1274	Peter de Ros	1482	Mag. Rob. Mome	1735	John Ewer
1287	Mag. Will de Filungele	1492	Mag. Sim. Stalworth	1753	Rich. Stevens
1322	Gilbut de Sandal	1511	Mag. Thos. Pert	1771	Geo. Turner
1323	Gilbut de Wygston	–	William Constable	1782	John Thoroton
1334	Adam de Stayngrave	–	John Whitinge	1821	Charles Roos Thoroton
1349	John de Cotyngham (or Codyngton)			1846	Frederic John Norman
1362	Henry de Codyngton			1889	Robert Manners Norman
1404	John Corby	1560	Robert Cressey	1895	Will. Vincent Jackson
1410	Thos. Clyff	1575	Robert Gibson	1918	Frank Robert Walford
1420	John Freman	1581	Mag. Sam. Fleminge	1943	Alfred T.G. Blackmore
1445	Rich. Bekyngham	1621	Francis Allen	1958 to 1959	George Cooper (interregnum)
1445	Gerald Herill	1624	Richard Langham		
1452	Hugh Cotes	1649	Thomas Whatton	1959	William N. Metcalfe
1452	Alexander Prowet	–	Thos. Robinson d.1657	1982	Kenneth A. Dyke
1471	Mag. Ralph Makerell	1662	Anthony Marshall		

The Bunker's Hill poor cottages.

LEFT: The Easthorpe cottage with mud walls. RIGHT: The pump and mud-built hovel of the Easthorpe cottage. CENTRE: Easthorpe cottages at the beginning of the century. BELOW: The cottages in 1989. OPPOSITE ABOVE: The Wyggeston cottages today. (HER) BELOW: A one-storey cottage in Queen Street, pulled down in the 1960s. (WJR)

ABOVE: A barn conversion on the Green: plays were performed here in the 19th century. (BH) BELOW: Dr Morgan outside the Easthorpe Manor Barn.

ABOVE: The date worked in header bricks in the Hollies farm in Easthorpe, 1807. RIGHT: The date worked in header bricks in Hospital Farm, Muston; 1807. CENTRE: Daniel Daybell, Dorking Poor — date stone in Church Farm, 1851 and date stone of BELOW: Dr Fleming's Hospital with Mrs Gilbert, a descendant of the Vincents.

ABOVE: The Witches of Bottesford in a 1620 chapbook.
(BPCC) BELOW: Early 20th century pensioners at the
Men's Hospital — the Earl of Rutland's almshouse.
(VC/BD) OPPOSITE: Men's Hopital accounts from the
1837 Charity Commissioners' Report. (LRO)

Each of the 17 receive the following monthly payments:—

	£.	s.	d.
In January	3	4	0
February	1	14	6
March	1	14	0
April	1	14	6
May	1	14	6
June	1	14	10
July 3d	1	14	0
„ 31st	1	14	0
August	1	14	0
September	1	15	4
October	1	14	6
November	1	14	0
December	1	14	6
Making the yearly allowance of each	£ 23	16	8

Every alternate Easter 14 pensioners receive a blue cloth gown of the value of 2l. 3s., and such as constantly reside are allowed whatever quantity of coals they require for their use, and also every species of necessary in the way of linen, bedding, and furniture.

A matron is attached to the establishment at an average salary of 15l. She cleans the house, cooks and washes for the pensioners.

One of the pensioners, for acting as porter, is allowed 10s. yearly ; and Thomas Oliver, the tenant of the Musson lands, 5s. for making up the accounts, and 2l. 4s. for paying the men.

The following are the receipts and expenditure of the charity from 1st January 1836 to 1st January 1837 :—

	£.	s.	d.
Balance of last account to 1st January 1836	1,245	13	1
One year's rental, due Michaelmas 1837	448	13	0
Interest on 764l. in the treasurer's hands	30	11	0
Samuel Wells, for the bark of five small oaks cut down towards the repairs of his outbuildings at Kettleby	1	10	0
	£1,726	7	1

Payments.

				£.	s.	d.
One year's monthly payments to the 17 hospital men, amounting to 23l. 16s. 8d. each, and 6l. 14s. 2d. to the matron				411	17	6
One year's casual payments (remainder of 28l. 14s. 9d.)				21	5	5

	£.	s.	d.			
Abatement of rent to Lady-day 1836 to Thomas Oliver	10	0	0			
Ditto to Samuel Wells	5	8	0			
				15	8	0

	£.	s.	d.
John Guy, for paint and painting the new cottage-house at Muston	1	17	6
Joseph and William Challands, for 1,000 drain-tiles used upon Thomas Oliver's farm at Muston in 1836	15	0	0
Thomas Harvey, gowns for 14 hospital men at Easter 1836	30	11	10
Messrs. Ridge, an account-book	0	4	0
Materials and labour for a new stable, cow-house, and calf-house on Samuel Wells's farm at Abkettleby	71	0	0
	567	4	3
Balance due to the hospital account 1st January 1837	1,159	2	10
	£1,726	7 ·	1

ABOVE: The Doom Painting, above the Victorian coat of arms and the nave (EAS) in BELOW: St Mary's Bottesford, here in 1845. (AE)

ABOVE: St John the Baptist, Muston in 1789. (JN)
LEFT: Datestone and Manners coat of arms
preserved at the Rectory in 1792. (JN) RIGHT:
The 1732 School House with the coat of arms in
situ. (JN) BELOW: Nichols' picture of the remains
of a building on charity land in the centre of
Bottesford. (JN)

ABOVE: The Bottesford School. (HER) LEFT: The Muston School, closed in 1962. (HER) RIGHT: Mr Ligonier's Parsonage building — Bottesford Rectory. BELOW: Muston Rectory. (HER)

LEFT: Muston Methodist Chapel: the original building was built 1802.
(HER) RIGHT: Bottesford Wesleyan Methodist Chapel of 1845,
converted by Mr W.J. Roberts into two houses in 1988. BELOW: The
rear of the Independent Salem Chapel in Albert Street.

ABOVE: The Baptist Chapel of 1789. BELOW: Buildings on the Wyggeston Hospital land in Church Street. (DB)

To Help One Another

The early 19th century prosperity of Bottesford, which is reflected in extensive building, was not easily apparent to the poorer sort in the 1830s. There were agricultural riots in 1830 as there were throughout the country: there had been 'breaking down and carrying the fences'. Parish officials paid £3 for the 'use and benefit of the fire engine about to be established at Grantham upon an improved principle', fearing haystack burning by farm labourers. On the other hand, building was going on apace: in 1831 Mr Barnsdale's new mill was assessed and an additional rate of 7s 6d placed upon each of the new brickyards. Bottesford families were encouraged to emigrate to save their being chargeable to the Parish. In 1832 Thomas Hardy and his wife had £10 paid for their passage to America; we are not sure they went, as a Thomas Hardy was appointed parish mole-catcher in February 1834, at the rate of £5 per annum. B. Challands and his wife were also advanced money, and a person was appointed or requested to see them abroad. Trouble persisted through the 1830s, and in 1835 there were 'cowardly attacks upon parish officers' property'. Clearly the strain of the ever increasing population was telling; in 1835 the parish officers offered £1 each to anyone prepared to emigrate, in addition to paying their fares. There were cuts in the pay of village labourers in 1835 and the following employers agreed only to employ Bottesford men: Richard Bartram, William Pickworth, Joseph Norris, John Hand, W. Lane, Challands, William Barnsdale, Daniel Guy, John Kettleborrow, Matthew Marshall, John Jarvis, George Willis, Thomas Spalton, Joseph Challands, William Daybell, Francis Orton, H. Sanderson, George Whitehead, Francis Vincent, John James and Francis Geeson.

While the parish endeavoured to control the poorer workers, they themselves undertook their own salvation. The 18th and 19th centuries saw an extraordinary development of self-help in all fields, but most especially in the ordinary sort of people developing their own clubs. In 1747 the Bottesford Friendly Benefit Society was established: it flourished through the 19th century, referred to in 1848 as the 'Old Village Club'. The members in 1845 held four meetings a year and paid 3s a quarter; when sick, 7s a week was paid. In 1792 there were 80 members who paid 8d a month and received benefit in time of sickness and distress: essentially this was a sick and burial club. Then there was the Odd Fellows Club, which was also a social club; on Whitsunday 11 June 1848, Rev F. Norman, the Victorian Rector of Bottesford and brother-in-law of the sporting 6th Duke, preached a special sermon for the Odd Fellows. On the following Thursday the Odd Fellows held their annual feast, a splendid celebration managed by the Secretary. The Odd Fellows particularly enjoyed the sermons by the Rector at the end of the century, Rev William Vincent Jackson, by which time there were 175 members. He was of the evangelical persuasion and roused everyone with his vivid exhortations.

There were various clothing and coal clubs; these tended to develop out of chapel and parish organisations, rather than from farmworkers' private initiatives. The Primitive Methodist clothing club's funds in 1857 amounted to £27, and 101 poor children received shoes and warm clothing out of this. The children themselves contributed 1d a week and the remainder was given by members and friends of the club. What these clubs suggest is that, through mutual self-help, Bottesford farmworkers assisted each other through the difficult farming times of the 18th and early 19th centuries. By the 1850s there was a more general feeling of wellbeing in the community; after the 109th Anniversary Dinner of the Friendly Society in 1856 the *Grantham Journal* village correspondent wrote 'all went cheerfully and quietly to their homes; it speaks much for the creditable estate of society in Bottesford when we can add that not a man was seen past his guard through intoxicating drinks'. By July 1856 the correspondent wrote 'few villages can boast of the wealth and influence that Bottesford can'.

Perhaps the most effective club in Bottesford's development was the Cow Club. The minute book, kept by the steward survives recording this Mutual Aid Society, set up by the smallholders of the Parish. The first rules of November 1814 relate to the stocking of the Inmeers pasture, land leased by the Duke to cottagers for the maintenance of their cows. The problem with enclosure was that farm labourers and cottages lost their grazing rights. The Bottesford solution was for the Duke to allocate land for the cottagers at a low rent. The cottagers organised the upkeep of the pastures: each year two stewards were chosen 'to look after the fences, mow the thistles, clean the drains or do anything requisite for keeping the pasture in a husbandlike manner'. The vital rule was 'any of the cottagers losing their cow by accident shall be entitled to five shillings from each person unless the cow hath been previously unhealthy or done with intent to defraud in which case they shall not be entitled to the benefit'. During the 1830s 'this last rule is expunged being superseded by the formation of the cottagers' society for the Mutual Assurance against losses of their cows'.

There survive lists of these cottagers, of which the two of 1829 and 1843 make a good comparison:

1829	1843	
Jonathan Singleton	1. Singleton	
Mr Walker	2. Piket	
Wm Robinson	3. Hardy	
Wm Robinson	4. Welbourn	
Elizabeth hallam	5. Guy	
Wm Leivesley	6. Rose	
Wm Farney	7. Winn	
George Winn	8. Miller	
David How	9. Miller	
Robt. White	10. Robinson	
Wm Challands	11. Robinson	
Silvester Bust – Mr Pool	12. Wilkinson	
Elizabeth Watts, Mr Wilkinson	13. Wilkinson	'the Above the preasent occupiers'.
Frances Rear	14. Challands Wm	
Mary Reynolds	15. Challands Wm	
Robt Pykitt	16. Challands Joseph	
Daniel Sissling	17. Hoe Thomas	
Edward Guy	18. Hoe David	
George Willson	19. Lievsley	
Elizabeth Buxton	20. Nixon	
Wm Pool	21. Halam	
Richard Hickson, Mr Nixon	22. Walker	
Richard Hickson, Mr Miller	23. Wilson	
Richard Hickson, Mr Miller	24. Wilson	

There were 24 cows allowed on this pasture from May to November, whereafter each cottager would graze two sheep from the end of November to the end of February.

The Cow Club was still in existence at the end of the 19th century. In 1899 the list of villagers who kept cows was recalled by Mr John Sutton, who was a young man at the time. The cow provided milk for cheese and butter and also for the pigs which each villager kept. A Pig Club also existed, naturally enough in any East Midland village at this time, but especially so in one which boasted the best pig breeder in England, Mr Daniel Daybell. The Bottesford Pig Club, founded in 1865, met at the school: in January 1886 there were losses due to swine fever, but all claims were met. These animals provided meat and the pig-killing was a great occasion. But the animals were also family pets, both cows and pigs, and they were well-fed and looked after.

The cow owners called in a cow-leech to give medicines to sick beasts: in the 1860s James Wilson was the village cow-leech. Horses were looked after by farriers, who not only shod the animal, but also administered pills and potions. James Morgan was the farrier in 1851; the blacksmith also helped look after horses and in 1851 Mrs Hannah James was the Easthorpe blacksmith. Numerous other people earned their living from these animals in the 1860s: the pig-jobber was William Colby, and he also dealt in cattle, as did John Parnham. George Sherwin made saddles and harness, and William Sutton was a fellmonger, presumably supplying John Sutton junior with skins for his glover's work. There were always butter dealers and factors, right up to the end of the century. Butter prices were controlled locally and it was Miss Geeson at the end of the century who set the price of butter for all the village in her shop in Church Street. But working for the score or so farmers in 1851, by far the largest occupational group were the agricultural labourers, 143 (10% of the population) in 1851 and 105 (8% of the population) in 1871. In Bottesford there is a revealing change in the structure of principal occupations between 1851 and 1871.

1851 (population 1,374)		*1871* (population 1,305)	
Agricultural labourers	143	Agricultural labourers	105
Scholars	117	Scholars	297
Servants	59	General servants	71
Lace Runners	35	No lace Runners	
Brickmaking or laying	27	Brickmaking or laying	11
Shoe making	26	Shoe makers	7
Farmer	26	Farmers	29
Farm servants	26	Farm servants	27
Railways	10	Railways	17

The biggest change is the huge increase in the numbers of children at school.

No wonder it was necessary to build the big new school opposite the Cross in 1854 at a cost of £900 and to extend it in 1878 at a further cost of £400. The Duke gave the land and his sister, Lady Adeliza Norman (who listed her occupation in 1871 as peer's daughter), and Rev F.J. Norman ensured that it was properly run. The school building was looked on very much as a village amenity. The Church Sunday School, the Bottesford Brass Band, the Friendly Society and the Odd Fellows Club all held meetings there. There were endless concerts, missions, addresses and temperance lectures. Gas was provided in the schoolroom by the Bottesford Gas Company, founded in 1865, so it was popular and there was an outcry when, in 1889, a new set of managers wished to charge one guinea a meeting. In a meeting there in December 1876 the Rector proposed the establishment of a local branch of the Church of England Temperance Society, to combat the effect of the public houses in the village. 'He strongly excited the risible faculties of the audience by relating an amusing anecdote of his relative, so well known by the familiar sobriquet of the Fighting Marquis of Granby, who when exhausted with long rides in the country used to call at the public houses and pour a quantity of brandy into each boot to cool his feet instead of imbibing it to cool his head'.

Canon Norman controlled the school, for 'his word was law'. The school logbook, begun according to the new regulations of the compulsory curriculum of the Revised Code in 1862, records his many visits and those of his wife, Lady Adeliza. The schoolmaster was clearly mortified on 23 March 1863 when 'Lady Norman visited the school this morning. School thin, Grantham Fair'. James Campkin was the master of the Free School at the time: expenses were £130 pa and 'were defrayed by income from land, by subscription and by the children's pence'. The mistress was Mary Norris. At the inspection carried out in connection with the new regulations of 1863 there were 49 pupils in the main school: 39 boys and 10 girls. Religious knowledge, compound multiplication and simple subtraction were tested and the Inspector was not too happy with the results. A change in teacher brought Mr Isaac Wildbore in 1864. He attracted new pupils, especially when Mr Gordon's academy closed and E. James and J. Goodson came in – numbers were up to 76, 60 boys and 16 girls. The curriculum of the junior children in 1864 was needlework, scripture and catechism, arithmetic, grammar, reading, copybooks, spelling and object lesson.

A major problem was attendance. In 1878 the schoolmaster recorded for 23 September 'attendance very poor – parents say shall not send children until after the Feast: gleaning not quite finished; infants kept till 5 pm to accommodate parents who wanted to glean'. On 4 October of that year there were a 'great many absentees owing to potato gathering'. Compulsory school attendance did not effectively come into schools until 1877 and the inspection revealed: 'lowest division a little weak but contains many backward children who have lately been brought in by operation of the education act'. The final move to successful full-scale education came in 1891: 'commenced on 19th October with Free Education, a great boon to the parents which I sincerely hope they will appreciate'. They did: the master, Mr Marston, recorded on 31 October 1891 'a considerable increase in the attendance'. The lads were taught such poems as *Horatius* by Lord Macaulay and Longfellow's *Killed at the Ford* and the songs included *Life is full of ups and downs* and *I'm a British boy, sir*. By the end of the century discipline was absolute under Mr Collett: 'order continues excellent' was the theme of the inspection.

But the village lads were not always perfectly behaved out of school – in January 1889 catapults were in action, breaking the windows of the curate's room and there was another shot into the police station. There was an undercurrent of ill-discipline in the village in spite of the police station, complete with cells, built in classical style in 1842. It was fortunate the police were available as there were frequent traffic accidents. In 1884 Mr Aukland of the Six Bells was driving a fare to Muston in his waggonette and collided with a trap driven by the son of Mr Furnivall, the Rector of Muston Mr Aukland was thrown out insensible and, whilst Mr Furnivall looked after him, his horse got loose, ran away and crashed into a trap driven by Mr Baker of Muston. Both Mr and Mrs Baker were thrown out and Mrs Baker fainted. In the same year, Inspector Allen's trap collided with a cart, and the other driver was 'inhuman and unfeeling enough to drive on'. There were many farming accidents: one was noted in 1889 when Mr James Furmidge, harvesting for Mr D. Daybell, fell from a load of corn and broke his collarbone. The *Grantham Journal* correspondent wrote that 'we deeply sympathise as he had a similar accident last year and as he is in no "club" it must be a serious loss to him'. One particularly unpleasant set of incidents happened in 1889, when there was a mysterious outbreak of dog-poisoning. Mr T. Hoe of the Easthorpe Sauce Works lost a dog who ate rabbit meat doctored with strychnine, and Mr R. Daybell of Easthorpe similarly lost a valuable shepherd dog. On 13 April there had been a mysterious case of cat poisoning, especially of some valuable cats belonging to Miss Curtis.

There was great tension in the village in 1876 when the new Newark-Melton railway line was being built: 'the advent of the navvy has been much dreaded by the nervous and timid, but . . . the labourers are of good character'. Canon Norman and Lady Adeliza had had experience of this before: in 1847 the Ambergate railway was being built and Mr Norman experimented: 'tried service in school for Railway Labourers – four came' and again on 25 July when none came. The situation was different by the 1870s and the 'contractors are careful to admit into their employ none but the better class of labourers'. On 5 August Mr Norman 'invited all workmen engaged on the new line to spend an hour or two visiting the Castle – 240 went, they were granted admission to the Castle, bread, cheese and a pint of beer per man. Some of the remarks on ''Bluff King Hal'' [the portrait of Henry VIII] were enough to provoke his picture to walk out of its frame'.

The strongest attempt to bring the labouring classes under control was the temperance movement. On 28 July Thomas Norris was fined for drunken driving of a horse. Great efforts were made to get people to drink other beverages; all kinds of threats abounded – it was reported on 11 August 1866 that the world would end on Thursday 16 August 1868, but nothing happened and drinking continued. Mr Norman's initiative of December 1876 proved successful, leading to the establishment of the Coffee House of 1881. According to Lady Adeliza's obituary in 1887 in the *Grantham Journal* the Coffee House 'distinctly owes its origin to her, the success of which – not as a financial venture – but as a means of overcoming evil with good, was always very near to her heart'. Great efforts were made to keep the Coffee House solvent: in March 1884 there was a concert for its benefit in the large schoolroom, with a programme 'attractive beyond all precedent, even in this proverbially musical village'. The Wesleyans and the Primitive Methodists had frequent public tea drinkings when money was raised for the Coffee House, but its 'expenses were heavy and profit unremunerative'. The second anniversary of the village branch of the YMCA was celebrated by a public tea at the Coffee House and Lady Adeliza Manners gave ½lb packages of tea to the poor on the occasion of her son's marriage.

The Bottesford Temperance Band was formed to 'discourse lively music' at village feasts and the Band of Hope linked with the Church Sunday Schools to organise a Flower Show. In 1889 the Reading Room of the Coffee House was enlarged to take 105 persons to serve as a parish tea room. A debate in the Bible Class in November 1889 discussed the Sunday closing of pubs – the miller, Mr Hickson opposed it; the proposer of Sunday closing suggested buying beer on Saturday, corking it, turning it upside down, then it wouldn't go flat! 38 were against Sunday closing, 23 for it: it was clear that the majority of Bottesford folk enjoyed their beer 'fresh from the cask' as Mr Hickson put it.

Perhaps what really brought about social control more than the schoolmaster, the police and the temperance meeting, were a number of organised pastimes as farm labourers began to have a little more leisure. Some became bellringers of the famous Bottesford St Mary bells, and in the evening, imitating the gargoyle on the south porch of the church, they rang handbells, obtaining a set in 1886. They played football in different village teams. Canon Norman's son, Rev Robert Norman, when he was curate and later rector, turned out for the Bible Class team. In October 1887 they played against the ironworkers of Messrs Hornsby's of Grantham. It proved a rough match; the Rector took exception to the language and insisted that one of the opponents should leave the field. The match was brought to a sudden end with Bottesford leading 4–1. The *Grantham Journal* correspondent commented: 'It is high time that football was played without the addition of strong adjectives'. The Bible Class cricket club beat the Grantham YMCA: 'last Saturday, some balls were stopped by that irresistible fielder ''Mr Grass'', which in many places was knee deep'. The Bottesford Cricket Club held its winter meetings at the Red Lion and made special arrangements with the GNR for late trains to stop at Bottesford after matches. The Bottesford Wanderers football side in 1884 was Martin, Sutton, Singleton, Daybell (Capt.), Hollingsworth, Wilkinson, Challands, Asher, James, Edwards and Tinley: they drew in December 2–2 with Barrowby Rovers. Another team in 1884 was Sherwin, Vincent, Hickson, Wood, Winn, Miller, Hickson, Padgett, Hollingsworth, Kettleborrow, Marston – they too drew 2–2 with the Vale of Belvoir; but Bottesford managed to beat Flintham in November 1884, 5–1.

Much of the activity of these clubs was educational. The YMCA had a rather unsuccessful series of lectures in 1884 on such diverse topics as 'Chinese Gordon', 'Birds, Insects and Flowers', 'The inspiration of the Bible', 'The early training of the young among the Jews', and The Life of the Prophet David'. There were choirs associated with all the chapels and the churches and in May the church choir gave a concert of glees, gavottes, songs and cantatas, listened to by 'altogether an audience the reverse of overwhelming' wrote the *Journal* correspondent. The Rector and Lady Adeliza looked after their choir: in January 1886 they offered a supper which was 'a sumptuous and bountiful repast – a variety of meats, game, plum-pudding, pasties etc – it was claimed that the organblower and the boys cried because they could not eat everything. On the basis "no song-no supper" a concert was given'. The sort of YMCA lecture which really brought in the crowds was Rev Henry Hewlett in 1886 on 'Railroads'. Rev Henry Smith's lecture later the same year met with tumultuous applause. He was a curate of Bottesford and he described his Alpine tour, 'dressed in costume worn in his mountain ascent – blue tunic coat, leggings, climbing boots and coarse straw hat, stout rope, trusty knife and strong axe'. The YMCA lectures with 'lime-light pictures on a screen' were also more successful than the Biblical ones. The final YMCA lecture of 1886 was 'Earthquakes and the Final Earthquake' and was followed by the hymn *Rescue the Perishing*.

It is possible to imagine an idyllic Bottesford in Victorian times, especially if one takes the *Grantham Journal's* correspondent as guide. At the Sunday School Anniversary in the Rectory in 1886 the children 'wandered at will along the cool margins of the river Devon which pursues its sinuous way through the shrubbery. Tea was taken under the Cedar tree protected from the fierce solar rays. The Rector and Lady Adeliza scattered nuts and sweets to be scrambled for. A monster balloon was released to end the evening and the children took home a substantial lump of rich plum cake'. Of course the daily reality was different. The cedar tree was thought to be dying in 1889 – it was called the 'wonder of Bottesford', but it is still alive 100 years after. There were quite appalling floods in the late 19th century: a hundred years ago the Devon and the Winterbeck flooded the High Street to a depth of two feet; at the Toll Bar, where it was five to six feet deep, the floods submerged a sweep's cart. But the worst difficulties were the severe times of the 1880s and '90s, when cold weather, heavy rains and a slump in farming *and* an industrial depression combined to bring real poverty to some of the poorer families. In 1887 the 'severity and long continuance of frost has intensified the distress which the labouring classes have patiently endured', wrote the *Grantham Journal*. 'The unemployed had a house-to-house collection which was very successful. The Rector gave coal and beef, Lady Adeliza bread, Rev Robert Norman beef'. In January the village charities were distributed. Eight widows received 15s each from Twinberry's charity. Thirty of the labouring classes were given 10s each from Bishop White's will, supplemented by £5 from the Rector. A loaf of bread was given to ten widows for ten weeks from Bend's Dole. The Duke's Dole of bread was given weekly to numerous recipients and each year the Duke gave a gift of blankets – in 1887 he gave 48 sheets, 12 blankets and 12 rugs to be distributed among the poor of the Parish. Things hardly improved during the 1890s: in 1896 we find Daniel Daybell distributing soup to 40 poor tenants from the Duke's charity. Coals were given out from a bequest of Miss Hough and the Hand charity began in 1891, by which some 20 or so deserving persons were given 10s each.

Clearly this village was still very much under the influence of the family at the Castle. Lady Adeliza, the Duke's sister, had an impact which is still remembered today, one hundred years after her death. She had married her cousin, Rev F.J. Norman, and he was recalled as 'tall as a guardsman, firm as a rock but at home in the humble cottage as he was in the gilded saloons of his patrician brother-in-law'. Lady Adeliza and Canon Norman left money for a charitable bequest of coals, which was distributed well into the 20th century. However, in 1909 a new means of support for village people was described by the Bottesford correspondent of the *Journal*. 'In January, 28 persons in the parish having satisfied the commissioners, presented themselves at the post office when total payments of approximately £6 10s 0d were given'. They were the first recipients of the state old age pensions of 5s a week, given to 70 year olds. In the same year, the Odd Fellows decided to dispense with their annual feast and Lloyd George said: 'we are lifting the shadow of the workhouse from the homes of the poor'.

The Bottesford Feasts

I think the best two days in the year which the people enjoyed most was the Thursday and Friday after the Whitsunday bank holiday; those was the days when the Oddfellows and Friendly Society held their annual club meetings. For several weeks people was preparing for it. The shop-keepers had to get in extra rations, the two Red Lion and Rutland Arms had to do extra brewing, scrubbing brushes was worn out by people cleaning their front door steps, flags was got out and put up, the Union Jack on a long pole tied to the cross, a large booth was put up in the Rutland yard the length of which is now the car park, and a smaller booth in the Granby yard, that was a smaller Club. The food for the meal was roast beef baked by Mr Martin in his back house opposite, vegetables done at the Rutland, cold apple pie and cream. Thursday was the special day, members who had left the village came to take part, and a good many wives with children in the pram, as they knew some relations would make them welcome. The gathering started at 11 o'clock in Queen Street, the crowd was a sight, everybody in their best clothes, the only day in the year some of the farm workers would dress up. One or two, I really did not know them, a good many in top hats, that gave a good many a good laugh, for some hats was too large, some had a small one, some was like a chimney pot straight, nothing mattered; that was a day for a top hat. Then there was the large banner, a lot of the members wearing rosettes, sashes, all a very grand sight. The secretary called out the names of the members, I don't think any one was missing, or the number of members say about 30 I don't know. Anyway the band strikes and the procession starts for the church, each man has his staff with the acorn on top. Arrive at the church the band each side of the path, while members walk in, the band stops before half are in, then Mr Moore starts a lively tune of the organ, the church is half full, the middle is kept for the members, it's just a short service and an address by the Canon, the singing of *Fight the good fight*. I can hear it now. The church bells did not ring, but a ringer rung the chimes, six bells rung by hand, they have done away with them now, you could play hymns on them. Back to the club from church; all go back to the booth for dinner, the band leading the way. After the meal of course, speeches. I have heard several talk about what took place; of course for several years they got Lord Cecil Manners for Chairman. He was member of Parliament so he had plenty to talk about, and tell them a few happy yarns. After his talk they gave him musical honours. The band starts playing, then all sing for he's a jolly good fellow. I should think before he speaks the secretary has to read out the balance sheet. I'm sure that would not take long, many would not understand it, but vote all in order and correct, cheers and drinks. Then other votes of thanks to the Duke of Rutland, the visitors and others with the band, then 4 o'clock all home for tea, all meet at the Cross at 5 o'clock, a parade round the village to the Rectory for photo taking, and a welcome to Canon Jackson and wife, and a great many who wished to do a little dancing. Then back to the booth for a social evening, singing and dancing, to end a very happy day for a good many.

Friday's Club was on a smaller scale, not such a large club, but carried on in the same way as the day before. The dinner was held in a booth in a yard at the back of the Granby in Queen Street; to keep us boys out the gates was closed and locked, members had to go through the front door. We did not mind, for during the three days, in Dan Daybell's stack yard and his paddock, was every kind of amusement, the only draw back was the shortage of pennies.

John Sutton (1890s)

1899 Cowkeepers in Bottesford

as written by *Mr John William Sutton (late of Swindon)*

People of Bottlesfor who oned cows

... *High Street* up to 1899

Mrs Barrand	Paper shop	2
Mr Sherwin	Rutland Arms	1
Mrs Parks	Post Office	3
Mrs Hallam		3
Mrs Anne Kettleborrow		4
Mrs Spalton		2
Mary Hannah James		1
Mr W. Parnham		2
Mr Welbourn		3
Mr R. Vincent		1
Mr W. Marshall		2
Mr J. Lenton		4
Mr J. Winn	Builders	1

... *The Nook*

Edward James	Milk to London
Tommy Jackson	

... *Albert Street*

Mr Tinley	2
W. Parnham	4
Mr C. Guy	1
Mr A. Guy	1
Mr Whittle	2

... *Queen Street*

Mrs George	Granby Inn	1
Mrs Wilkinson		3
Mr Marriott		1

J. Hudson	2
J.D. Robinson	2
Coffee House	2
The Bull	1

... *Chapel Street*

Mr H. Challands	2
Mr Singleton	4

... *The Green*

T. Norris	4
Mrs Dickson	2

... *Market Street*

J. Hardy		2
G. Goodson		1
Mrs Polly Norris		1
J. Sutton		1
D. Daybell		4
Mr B. Orton	Milk to London	

... *Bunkers Hill*

B. Hollingworth	4
S. King	4

... *Easthorpe Lane*

G. May		4
H. Challands		1
G. Exton		3
W. Waide		2
G. Rimmington		2
H. Norris		2/3
H. Tomlinson	Muston Lane	3

I do not know about: C. Hickson or Headly Miller

Bottesford Brass Band lead the 1911 Coronation Celebrations. (DB)

94

LEFT: Mr William Sutton, Bandmaster, and Dr Shepherd with prize
pike from the canal. (DB) RIGHT: Mr William Sutton and his son, Mr
John Sutton. (DB) BELOW: Supplying the milk. (DB)

Theatre, Bottesford

For the Benefit of

MR. WATSON;

Who humbly solicits the support of the Inhabitants of Bottesford & its Vicinity.

On Saturday Evening, May 19th, 1827,

Will be performed Goldsmith's celebrated Comedy of

She Stoops to Conquer,

Or, The Mistakes of a Night.

Hardcastle...Mr. KENNEDY   Young Marlow...Mr. SPENCER
Hastings...Mr. WATSON   Tony Lumpkin...Master KENNEDY
Diggory...Mr. LESTER   Roger...Mr. MARTIN
Mrs. Hardcastle...Mrs. SPENCER Miss Hardcastle...Mrs. KENNEDY
Miss Neville...Miss KENNEDY

End of the Play the following Entertainments.

A COMIC SONG, Mr. SPENCER.

A Comic Song, Master Kennedy.

To conclude with the Laughable Farce of

THE REVIEW

Or, Wags of Windsor.

Deputy Bull,...Mr. KENNEDY
Captain Beauguard,......Mr. WATSON
Loony Mc' Twolter,...Mr. SPENCER
John Lump...Master KENNEDY
Grace Gaylove...Mrs. SPENCER   Lucy...Miss KENNEDY

Tickets to be had of Mr. Watson.

To commence at Half-past Seven o' Clock.

PIT—1s.   GALLERY—6d

Langley, Printer, Bookbinder, and Paperhanger, Mansfield.

LEFT: Philip Palmer of Church Farm, soon after 1902. (CP) RIGHT: playbill from 1827 — the Theatre was the Barn on the Green. The rear of the playbill shows a recipe for a sick cow. (DB)

LEFT: Lady Adeliza Norman. (DB)
RIGHT: Rev F.J. Norman. (DB)
BELOW: A funeral procession early in
the 20th century. (DB)

ABOVE: The old Hand's cottages. (DB) CENTRE: Market Street. (DB)
BELOW: Albert Street. (DB)

GREAT NORTHERN RAILWAY.

BELVOIR CASTLE.

CHEAP EXCURSION TICKETS

WILL BE ISSUED TO

BOTTESFORD

FROM

Burton, Derby, Ilkeston, Basford, Nottingham, Melton Mowbray, and Leicester,

AND TO

REDMILE AND HARBY AND STATHERN

From Melton Mowbray and Leicester.

Also from Lincolnshire and Yorkshire.

Particulars may be obtained at Stations, or from
G. J. GIFFORD, Esq., District Manager,
Nottingham (Telephone No. 299)

Tickets of Admission to the Castle can be obtained at Redmile or Bottesford Stations at 3d. each.

Belvoir Castle is open to the Public on Week-days, from 10 a.m. to 5 p.m.

The Mill, Belvoir Road,

BOTTESFORD.

MRS. RAITHBY.

Teas Provided on Application.

The village in 1902 — shops and holiday premises. (VC)

CYCLISTS' HARBOUR!

JAMES MILLER'S
Refreshment Rooms.

Good Accommodation for Motorists and Cyclists.

SPACIOUS ROOMS FOR VISITORS.
PRIVATE LAWN AND GARDEN.

 Large and small parties catered for.

THE FERNS, HIGH ST.,
BOTTESFORD.

VISITORS TO BELVOIR CASTLE.

Belvoir Coffee House
 # Refreshments Rooms,

BOTTESFORD.

**Large and small parties Catered for.
Good Accommodation for Cyclists.**

LARGE ENCLOSED YARD.

*Schools and Choir Parties Catered for on most
Reasonable Terms.*

SIX BELLS INN,

BOTTESFORD, NOTTS.

W. LAMB, Proprietor.

Pleasure Parties for Belvoir Catered for
on the Shortest Notice.

Brougham, Waggonette, and
Horse and Trap for Hire.

Good Accommodation for Cyclists
and Week-end Visitors.

TERMS MODERATE.

DEVON FARM,

Bottesford, Notts.

MRS. F. B. LANE.

Superior Private Apartments with or without Board.
Near Station.—Terms on Application.

MRS. J. D. BEND,
The Willows,
Easthorpe, Bottesford,

Comfortable Private Apartments.
Terms on Application.

Comfortable Private Apartments,
with or without Board.

For Terms, apply to

MISS M. H. JAMES,
HIGH STREET, BOTTESFORD.

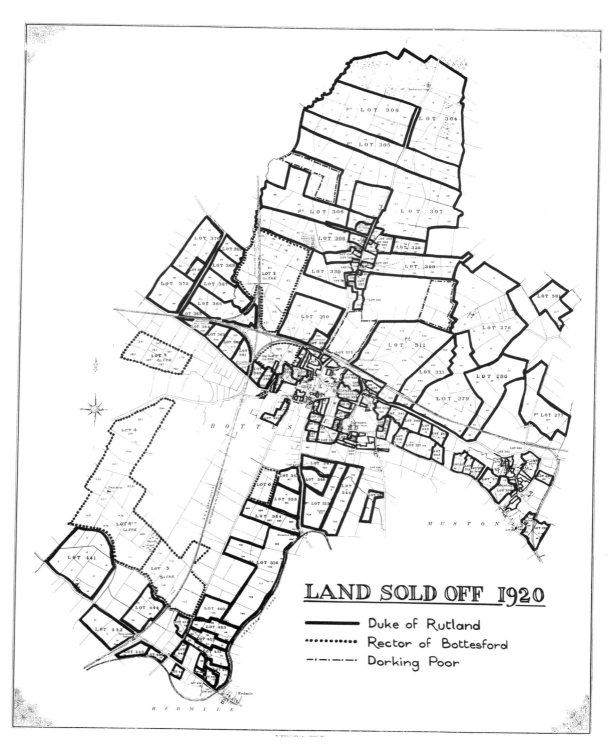

LAND SOLD OFF 1920

———————— Duke of Rutland

·············· Rector of Bottesford

—·—·—·— Dorking Poor

The Duke's Sale map. (UPT)

102

The Duke's Sale

In March 1920 the 8th Duke of Rutland sold 2,066 acres of Bottesford Parish. In April 1920 Rev Frank Walford, Rector of Bottesford, sold off around 545 acres of glebe land in Bottesford parish. In July 1920 the Trustees of the Dorking Charities in Surrey sold 143 acres, being the Dorking Poor Estate in Bottesford Parish. Why were 2,750 acres, 55% of the total parish acreage, suddenly sold off?

The simple answer is that the village had changed. At the beginning of the twentieth century the farming land still remained largely pasture, but a good proportion of the sandy loam land had turned over to market gardening, with two large nurseries or vineries. Large quantities of flowers and fruit were produced in 1900. Arum lilies, chrysanthemums and roses were grown. Strawberries were produced as early as March and April; grapes, tomatoes and cucumbers were cultivated by W.A. Robinson at the Belvoir Road Nurseries and Mr Page at the Nottingham Road Nurseries. Bottesford had become a holiday village, with hundreds of visitors at bank holidays – 700 came by train on the Whit Bank Holiday, 1902. In May 1909, 100 clerical staff from London King's Cross station travelled to Bottesford and had a substantial cold lunch at the Rutland Arms. The Coffee House, run by John Hardy for 33 years, had become a refreshment room, offering accommodation for 'cyclists. In addition to these market gardening and holiday ventures, the farmers had by 1909 successfully joined together to produce local cheese at the Cheese Factory in Queen Street. Farm labourers were renting allotments from the Parish Council. Physically, however, the village around the time of the First World War was little changed from when it experienced the great building boom of the early 19th century – a Bottesford man who lived in Sheffield returned in 1914 after 30 years' absence and said the village was quite unspoilt; he felt great peace and contentment.

It was the Great War which changed everything. The Feasts, the club shows, the flower shows – all had to be suspended. Great efforts went into raising money and produce for soldiers and sailors. The Bottesford Brass Band, after many years of success under William Sutton, was led by Mr Pacey, and they provided dance music for a successful whist drive and dance for Red Cross Funds in January 1915. Eggs were collected by the hundred for convalescent soldiers. Gradually the reality of war seeped through; even the anodyne pages of the *Grantham Journal* failed to hide the suffering. In February 1915 the population was given instructions as what to do in case of invasion. Fred Shaw, who worked for Mr Philip Palmer at the Dorking Poor Farm, was the first Bottesford man to die; 30 more were killed. Mrs Jallands of Easthorpe had four sons at the front, one of whom, Ernest Jallands, won the MM early on and was wounded. He had stopped a runaway team of horses and then later saved his gun, although most of the horses were killed by a shell. Mr Burroughs from Rectory Farm was blinded, and both Mr H. Brewster and Mr Frank Allcorn were so badly wounded they took postmen's jobs after the war, unable to continue farming. There was a Zeppelin raid on Nottingham but it did no damage to Bottesford.

While the war was a disaster for individuals, farmers made better profits. One in particular, Mr G.E. Marsh from Nottinghamshire, took advantage of the farming subsidies and developed his land. Tractors appeared; in 1918 the Burroughs at Rectory Farm had one in use, a Titan. Mr Daniel Daybell continued to win prizes at the Royal Show. The Leicestershire War Agricultural Committe subsidised the distribution of seed potatoes. Sugar was distributed by the Government for fruit growers. Small boys earnt themselves a few pence by destroying sparrows, 6d a dozen for old birds, 3d per dozen for young birds and 1d for six eggs. The lads were even able to turn the old conker tradition to use as the school encouraged the collection of horse chestnuts for oil. The war brought security of tenure for tenant farmers and cottagers in a way only dreamt of in the past; this was the major change in agricultural districts as a result of the First World War.

The Rent Restriction Act of 1915 kept rents down. This legislation was essential at the outbreak of the war, as house building stopped and all kinds of prices shot up – witness the postcard sent from Bottesford on 7 August 1914. 'Isn't it awful. Everything is dreadfully dear here'. The attempts to control increases in rents succeeded and, in the aftermath of the war, regulations were consolidated into the Increase of Rent and Morgage Interest (Restrictions) Act of 1920. Perhaps here we have the reason for the great nationwide sales of land in 1920. There was a boom throughout the country in 1919 and landowners, not easily able to raise rents, decided to sell.

The Duke was open about his situation. By November 1919 he had made up his mind to sell and he spoke to his tenants at a meeting in Woolsthorpe, which was reported in detail in the *Grantham Journal* of 8 November 1919. 'He was no longer a young man, but he could honestly say that never in all his life had he taken a step which was so hateful to him. He felt it terrible and nothing but the force of circumstances could have made him do what he was doing. As a consequence of the War, the pressure of taxation and the great increase in expenses in countless ways, had left no option to many landowners; it was simply impossible to go on. He was not grumbling but those were the facts, and so after many months of anxious consideration with other members of the family he had decided to part with a portion of the estate in order that he, and those who came after him, might still continue to live at Belvoir'.

The sale took place over several days at the Corn Exchange in Melton Mowbray in March 1920. The parishes of Waltham, Thorpe Arnold, Goadby Marwood, Easton, Stathern and Hose were sold 'practically in their entirety'. Major portions of Granby, Plungar, Muston and Bottesford were sold. The land raised £438,354 and the timber £10,596. Those tenants who could afford it took out mortgages to buy their farms. Mr Daniel Daybell bought his, Mr Barnes bought Normanton Lodge, where he had been tenant, Mr W. Love bought his Normanton Farm and Mr Hickson bought Easthorpe Mill where his family had been for 150 years. Mr Allen bought his property, then known as Allen's Tea Gardens as Hoe's were no longer producing their range of sauces and chutneys. Two attractive Victorian cottages on the east side of Albert Street went for £370 the pair. Mr A.E. Taylor bought his butcher's shop on the Market Place. The schoolmaster's house in Grantham Road was sold for £700. The ten Bunker's Hill cottages went to Mr Winn for £380. Nearly 80 years later, Bottesford people still speak of the Duke's sale; the fact that such sales were happening nationwide did not alter the huge impact of this particular local event. When, in the same year, the Rector, on the instructions of the Peterborough Diocese, sold most of his glebe land, including the Rectory Farm and Debdale Farm to Messrs Burrows, and the Dorking Parish trustees sold their farm to Mr Philip Palmer, the whole basis of local property ownership had changed. Henceforth most tenant farmers were owners, although the Duke retained a number of farms in the south of the Parish. He also retained Hospital Farm in Muston and Sands Farm in Bottesford.

The new owners set to, draining some land, although money became short with heavy mortgage payments. On the whole, in the twenties and thirties, farmers reverted to pasture farming, except on the good sandy soil in the centre of the Parish. Oats were grown for horses, who worked the farms. Lincoln Red cattle were fattened on the pasture and, together with Shorthorns, provided milk. Leicestershire-Lincolnshire Cross sheep were reared for wool and meat. Barley was grown and some of this was fed to pigs as mash. The surplus milk went to young pigs. Sheep were folded on turnips and mangels, which grew well on the sands, although better still if the land was drained. Linseed was grown for cattle cake. Profits were limited, and tended to depend on the size of the milk cheque, first from the big London and Nottingham dairies and then, after 1935, from the Milk Marketing Board. The cheese factory in Queen Street did not last long, closing in the twenties. Times were difficult for there were fewer farm labourers, tempted by the slightly better wages of Grantham, and still able to live in the village because of the railway. Mr George Marsh became the largest landowner farming in the village, with over 700 acres, which he worked effectively.

In some ways life in Bottesford in the 1920s and 1930s reverted to its pre-war pace. The village girls went around on Mayday with May garlands. The village library, first established in the 1870s, was kept going in the school, first by the Parish Council and then in 1929 it was handed over to the County Council. Instead of the Duke's tenant farmers meeting him for an annual dinner, the Farmers' Union established its own dinner at the Rutland Arms. The village happily reverted to its status as a holiday centre: the May Bank Holiday in 1920 reminded 'people of the Bank Holidays of 20 years before, as 700 people came in by train'. On that day the Normanton level-crossing keeper had a busy time, with 60 cars, 40 other vehicles and 500 'cyclists. The schoolmaster in 1902, Mr Victor Collett, had written *How to spend a holiday in the Vale of Belvoir* and this was reprinted by Harrison's of Grantham as *A Guide to Belvoir, Bottesford and District*; several village shopkeepers took advertisements. Three tea shops offered, in the words of the Coffee House proprietor, 'a right good spread at little cost'. W. Samuel sold postcards of the village, little realising he was starting a trade which today sees his old cards fetch prices of up to £10 each. The Post Office was run by the Silverwood family; Lieutenant Silverwood had been a PoW in Germany. The Co-op was re-established in Queen Street: it had started in the 1890s at the eastern corner of Chapel Street and Queen Street. There were several shops in High Street and more in Market Street. The butchers in the 1920s were Goodsons in Queen Street, Robinsons, later Goodsons, in Market Street, Taylors at the Cross and Millers, later George, in High Street. As today, however, the shops come and go, and it is impossible to reconstruct an accurate account; the most significant shopkeepers were the Co-op in Queen Street, Messrs Sutton in High Street, Samuel in Market Street next to Moulsher, Miller in High Street, Winn (the draper) in Queen Street, and the Misses Geeson in Church Street.

By far the most important professional men were the doctors. A purpose-built surgery and residence called Beechwood was constructed in the High Street in 1903 for and by Dr Glover. He left the village during the First World War. There was a practice at the Thatch with Dr Wills, Dr Martin and Dr Hamilton; Dr Shepherd, a great fisherman, lived in the large house, Greenfields, at the beginning of Belvoir Road.

Schooling continued exactly as before the Great War, with most village children going to the school by the Cross. Some of the farmers sent their children to Miss James' school in Queen Street, where the curriculum and discipline were strictly imposed. Miss Nellie James and her sister were important village residents at Woodbine Cottage: Miss James started collecting for Dr Barnardo's at the age of 12 and continued for the next 70 years. Some of her scholars, like Mr G.E. Marsh's son, Philip Marsh, went on to the Magnus Grammar School. Before the

Great War, the best secondary school closest to Bottesford was Sedgebrook School, conveniently at the next stop on the GNR line, and the lads who went there were known as the Sedgebrook Sugar Suckers. But this school was a casualty of the Great War and so the village's secondary schooling centred on Melton Grammar School, also accessible by train in the 1920s.

Most services were locally provided in those years. The milk was brought round on a bicycle by Roland James and then by Mr Jackson. Water was obtained either from your own well or from the one-hundred or so pumps. There was a water cart which brought water from the river for gardens and plants, and for flushing drains. There was no mains sewage: the cesspits were regularly emptied by the 'honey cart' men! The Parish Council, of which Mr Daniel Daybell was clerk for 30 years, maintained most services such as the Washdyke for cleaning sheep, superintended by Mr James. The Cross and Stocks were frequently repaired and the village dump, suggested in 1925 and set up in 1927 by the railway crossing, was the source of much complaint. There was a determined but unsuccessful effort to get a subway built under the line by the Normanton level crossing – an indication of the considerable number of trains.

Of course a memorial for the soldiers of the Great War was of great significance, and in June 1919 it was decided in principle to establish a village hall. In April 1919 the school was given a small German machine gun as a memorial. Then in May, the Parish Council received a letter from the War Trophies committee offering the village a German field gun and carriage. In October 1919 a site for the gun opposite the hospital was agreed upon and the owner, Mrs Simpkins, was granted a rent of 1s a week. In 1925 Mr Standley bought the land and asked for the gun to be removed. By now it was an embarrassment, and the Parish Council offered it to the British Legion who accepted it, removed it and it quietly disappeared.

In 1931 electricity was brought to the village. By this time the Parish Council had prevailed upon the Rural District Council to build council houses in Belvoir Road, constructed with pigsties for farm labourers to develop their own strain of Large Whites. The village was settled by the 1930s into a peaceful routine, with Gilbert and Sullivan operas as an annual event.

Bottesford and Muston population

	Bottesford	Muston		Bottesford	Muston		Bottesford	Muston
1086	500	not known	1801	804	204	1871	1315	353
1377	450	140	1811	891	226	1881	1331	312
1563	550	150	1821	1070	242	1891	1286	290
1603	650	160	1831	1320	300	1901	1221	268
1670	800	220	1841	1375	351	1911	1174	262
1742	772	180	1851	1374	411	1921	1204	261
			1861	1415	360	1931	1093	218
						1951	Bottesford and Muston joined together Total 1481	

1036-1742 figures are estimates; 1801-1951 figures are from the National Decennial Census.

Life during the First World War

When my family went to live in Bottesford in the year 1913 it was the village which seemingly had everything. It must have been almost self-supporting. Here is a record of the many amenities of that well stocked village. It had a carpenter, builder, tailor, two dressmakers, blacksmith with his forge, no spreading chestnut tree for him. It had a bede house for men and Dr Martin with his surgery. There were two schools, one private and the other Church of England. It had two vineries, windmill and watermill, both working, a cheese factory, stables, tea-gardens, gasworks, three butchers, each with their individual slaughter house, saddler, three bakers, each baking their own bread etc, three boot and shoe repair shops. It had a taxi service run by Mr Singleton with horses and carriages and Mr Samuel, the village carrier. There were three chapels, all of them functioning, the Wesleyans in Chapel Street, the Primitive Methodist very dear to me, tucked away on the Village Green, and the Baptist Chapel in Queen Street, which eventually became a war casualty. There was the beautiful Anglican Church presided over by Canon Jackson, whose only son was killed in the war, and the Curate, Rev Bennett, who later when he retired came back to live in Bottesford, I believe. There were four public houses, a lending library in a loft and ten shops of varying kinds. The river Devon, where we paddled, flowed through the village and the horses and carts splashed through the ford. There was the Winterbeck where we took our jam jars and nets, and caught tiddlers and tadpoles and the canal which we loved, with its occasional horse drawn coal barges and a towpath on which we could walk for miles. Opposite the Market Cross stood the Church of England School adorned with Queen Victoria Jubilee Clock, where I received my bit of education. The primary departments were taught by Miss Williams and Miss Osborne and the older children by Miss James, Miss Gilding, Mrs Daybell (Julia, as we called her behind her back), and the headmaster, Mr Victor Collett (whom we called 'the old boss'). There were two railway stations for Bottesford was a junction, but one of the stations was not in use, and there was the police station, where we lived. It had one small and one large prison cell, complete with central heating and flush lavatories. We in the police house had neither. Our prisoners were chiefly deserters from the armed forces and poachers, with their loot; and I think we must have shared their loot, for I remember we had quite a few meals of rabbit, hare, partridge and pheasant. I have never tasted pheasant since those days. We were the first house to have the telephone installed. We were Bottesford 2 and the Post Office was Bottesford 1. During the dark days of the 1914-1918 war my sister and I delivered newspapers night and morning for four years, and we knew virtually everybody and every house in the village. I may have missed out other worthy members of our village community, including the Town Crier with his bell and loud 'Oh Yez' giving us vital information of one kind or another, and always finishing off with the formulae, 'God Save our King and Country'; after all there was a war on. And all around us we had the free and uncluttered countryside overlooked by the majestic Belvoir Castle on the southern horizon. About the only traffic through the village was an occasional horse and cart and during the war, exciting to us children, marching tramp of soldiers on their way to Grantham or Nottingham, and sometimes stopping in our green fields for rest and refreshment. I lived in Bottesford for nearly eight years, until 1921, when we came to live at the police station in Melton Mowbray, but I left part of myself in Bottesford and went back quite often to roam its streets, lanes and fields again, later taking my husband and children with me to picnic in some of my still remaining childhood hideouts. I seldom go there now. It is no longer my village. But it still remains in my mind a sweet and blessed memory.

Mrs Jordan, née Smith

LEFT: Mr Harold Brewster before he was wounded in the Great War. (DB) RIGHT: Mrs Brewster and her London cousin 1910. (DB) BELOW: Mr T. Samuel by the German gun in the 1920s. (DB)

ABOVE: Taylor's butcher's shop. (B) CENTRE: A group of school
children early in this century. (DB) RIGHT: Canon Vincent Jackson.
BELOW: Queen Street in the 1920s. (PM)

ABOVE: Acacia House was bought by Mr George Marsh in the Duke's sale, and Mr A. Marsh lives there today. BELOW: Miss James' school, dressed up for Empire Day in the 1920s. (GC)

LEFT: Village schoolchildren maygarlanding in the 1930s. (DB)
RIGHT: Brownies in the 1920s. (DB) BELOW: Scouts early in the 20th
century, with the schoolmaster's house in the background. (IK)

ABOVE: Scouts early in the 20th century. (IK) BELOW: Cyclist in High
Street with tea shop. (PM)

PREFACE.

Dear Reader,

The great success and cordial receptions which have attended the previous editions of my Cookery Book have encouraged me to compile this further Edition, which is considerably larger and contains many new and up-to-date recipes.

During recent years the cost of living has greatly increased and many ladies have sought a cookery book giving recipes which, whilst ensuring dainty, wholesome and nourishing dishes, are withal modest in cost. My Cookery Book will be found to meet these requirements.

The increasing sales of my work throughout the country lead me to think that the Book meets a want in all middle-class homes, and I have every confidence that you will find it of great usefulness.

With kind remembrances to my friends and students.

Yours sincerely,

HESTER H. TUXFORD, M.C.A.

" Southbourne,"
Bottesford,
Notts.

LEFT: Miss Tuxford's cookery book. (CC) RIGHT: Mr Frank Jackson
on his milk round in 1936. (JC)

ABOVE: A Palmer wedding during World War I, 1916. (CP) BELOW:
Mr and Mrs Cyril Palmer's wedding in 1938. (CP)

Village shops in the 1920s.

ABOVE: The Friendly Society process to church in the 1920s. (GC)
BELOW: Dr Glover's surgery. RIGHT: Floods by the Church in 1937.

The Impact of War

By 1942 Bottesford must have felt like the front line in total war. A searchlight group was established at Normanton, there was an Ack-Ack battery nearby on the Elton Road, a huge RASC petrol distribution centre was established and a major Bomber Command aerodrome was fully operational, sending Manchester, and then Lancaster bombers across the North Sea. On the night of 8 May 1941, German bombers dropped 171 high explosives and many incendiary bombs on the area between Normanton and Plungar, and the signalman, Mr Gamble, was nearly blown out of his signalbox. Winston Churchill, in his memoirs, *The Second World War*, referred to the raid, suggesting that in fact the target was Nottingham. 'Through our own interference with the German radar beams' the bombs fell short of the target and 'were dropped in open country, with the total casualties of two chickens'. No one knew that then. The reality of modern warfare continually came home to Bottesford people. Two red electric lights were erected by the RAF at the top of St Mary's steeple; they could be seen far across country: a welcome beacon for 'planes returning from raids, put there to prevent them from crashing into the steeple, immediately due south and in the direct line of the major runway.

In many respects the nation was ready for war in 1939 – civilians were prepared for gas attacks, men had trained in Territorial Army units, the nation was to some extent rearmed and the War Department had plans for military and air bases through the country. The construction of an Army camp to the west of the village, between the Newark-Melton railway and the Orston Lane level crossing, happened almost overnight. Requisition notices taking over farming land were given to farmers the day before work started. The railway junction proved strategically valuable for petrol supply, and the distribution camp sited at the junction could take in and send out petrol north, south, east and west. The RASC camp, No 17 Petrol Depôt, was a huge affair, with at least 10 officers and 120 other ranks: there were well over 100 huts of all shapes and sizes, extensive storage tanks and vehicle maintenance workshops. The function of the camp was to store and distribute petrol, the nucleus of success for the mobile armies of a modern war. Early on an excellent German design for a petrol can, the 'Jerrycan', had been copied. These were manufactured in bulk at the Raleigh factory in Nottingham and brought to Bottesford for filling and transhipment to motorised army units. Men of the Pioneer Corps did much of the tough and dangerous work involved. There were three mobile fire-fighting units at the camp: everyone knew the danger. But the men themselves were young and lively and they made a strong impression on local people. Some had passes to live in village houses, and found their way to work by bike. Controls were extremely strict, for petrol was tightly rationed and few could use cars. The camp astride the Orston Road cut local access to Orston village.

The camp drew its water from the Whatton camp in case of fire; it had a cinema and extensive NAAFI facilities. There were extensions of the main line sidings and, in addition, a narrow-gauge railway connected the standings for petrol cans and tanks to the sidings. The rails of these specially constructed lines ran in cuttings, safer from explosion and enemy attack. Local people say today that the German propaganda broadcasts by William Joyce, Lord Haw-Haw as he was called, claimed the camp was successfully destroyed by the Luftwaffe. This was not true, but arose perhaps from RAF decoy fires, established in the Vale of Belvoir to distract and disinform the enemy.

Partly as a result of the camp, the railway became extremely busy. The movement of petrol to supply jeeps, three-ton trucks, tanks and 'planes was clearly the lifeline which kept transport moving, but the steam-powered locomotives of the Government-controlled railway system were part of an extraordinarily complex war. Bottesford felt this as trains moved through day and night. Yet, alongside all this high technology, Bottesford villagers had no running water and still relied on pumps, wells and water butts, taking water from their roofs. They used bikes for transport. as did everyone else; by the end of the war even airmen were issued with bikes. But it was not easy negotiating village rural roads in the blackout, unless you happened to be near the camp, which was brilliantly lit if there were no enemy air movements. The Rector, Rev Frank Walford, rode all round the Parish, often wearing his straw hat – he was a quiet and well-loved man. The Methodist Minister at the time, Rev Philip Foster, remembers 'cycling at night by faith and by smells – the bean fields had a particularly fragrant aroma, and the ducks and pigs were easy to identify. Flt Sgt George Hawes, the Australian pilot, got round by bike too, enjoying his rides around the countryside. His great friend and air gunner, a Canadian, Flt Sgt Bill Blair, first learnt to ride one at Bottesford. George Hawes wrote that 'gangs of us do a bit of bike riding after tea. The roads are wonderful and it is really enjoyable'. He 'cycled into Newark to the May Fair and to the swimming pool.

These airmen were with 207 Squadron RAF, the first operational squadron to fly from Bottesford Aerodrome in November 1941. For some time before that the airfield was under construction by Wimpey; many of the men who built the runways and the camp were Irish, and they were billeted in the village for many months. It was a major construction exercise, especially as heavy clays made work extremely difficult. There was mud everywhere: one of 207 Squadron's wireless operators, Sgt Joseph Scott, described it graphically: 'When we got to Bottesford I was appalled by the mess. It was a newly constructed airfield and there was mud from one end to the other! We lived in mud, we walked in mud, we cycled in mud, we took off in mud, we landed in mud', he wrote.

But the camp had facilities not available to the villagers, in particular tap water and sewerage. Gradually it became a small town which, by the final years of the war, housed over 2,000 men and women, complete with extensive mess halls, gymnasia, a squash club, a cinema and gigantic hangars. These could hold enormous numbers of people and in 1943 Gracie Fields came. Lt Moss from the RASC camp 'cycled over to hear her and recalls her appearance before a vast audience. When presented with a microphone, she said 'we shan't be needing this'.

When 207 Squadron first flew from Bottesford it was equipped with two-engined Manchester bombers. These were brought into operational service during early 1941 and flew from Bottesford from November 1941 to April 1942. This 'plane was the immediate predecessor of the Lancaster. It was tested partly by 207 Squadron at Boscombe Down and, when flown by experienced pilots who knew how to nurse the Vulture engines; it was a success. But some pilots experienced trouble with overheating, the curse of the Manchester. Accordingly the AV Roe bomber designers reverted to the well-tried Merlin engine, also used on the Spitfire and, by giving the 'plane a wingspan of 102 feet, made four engines possible — thus was born the Lancaster.

Lancasters started flying from Bottesford in May 1942, after 207 Squadron had converted during March and April. There followed a period of intensive flying as the new bombers made their presence felt. It was then that Air Vice Marshall Harris took over Bomber Command and developed his policy of area bombing, partly to destroy German industry and partly to destroy civilian morale. Arguments rage today among historians about the success and morality of this saturation bombing, which the Lancasters and the extraordinary courage of their air crew made possible. George Hawes wrote in March 1942. 'I have been transferred onto four engine bombers now. They certainly are wizard kites and we should give the Jerries 'ell this Summer'. 207 Squadron from Bottesford did just that, dropping a record 317 tons of bombs during the month of July 1942.

But at what a cost! As the summer months of 1942 dragged on, the people of Bottesford had to cope with awful news. Singapore had been captured in February 1942, with the loss of thousands of British troops. The Army in North Africa, under Auchinleck, could not cope with Rommel and was in danger. Renewed Luftwaffe raids in early 1942 threatened the locality — there was a bad attack on Grantham in January. And now, as the night-flying Lancasters took off, so the villagers, often counting them back in during the early hours of the morning, realised that some men they saw in the village one day, and welcomed into their own homes, might not return the next. In early June W/O Wathey's plane was missing after a raid over Essen. This was the immediate follow-up to the second of the two huge 1,000 bomber raids, set up by Bomber Harris to terrify the Germans. All the 'planes from Bottesford on the first 1,000 raid on Cologne on 30/31 May had returned, as had those which took part in the next one on Essen on 1/2 June 1942. During June 1942 George Hawes flew seven operational flights, mostly in Lancaster No R5632, N for Nuts, including the third 1,000 bomber raid, on Bremen on 25/26 June.

Another 207 Squadron pilot, Bob Weatherall, also kept a diary, and he was a great friend of George Hawes. They both recorded the welcome they received from villagers. They were particularly friendly with Mr and Mrs Brown; she was the schoolmistress at Muston and, like so many others, welcomed the home-sick airmen to their homes. Bob Weatherall wrote in his diary for 28 June 1942 'Got George to come over to Brown's with me. Played crib with Pop. Had a few shots with the gun and lounged around in general. George seemed to enjoy himself very much.'

George's air gunner, Bill Blair, liked to visit the Doubleday family at their home in the High Street. Rev Philip Foster remembers Sgt Blair sitting quietly, reading in the front room, appreciating the home-from-home offered him by a Bottesford family aware of how far from home in Saskatchewan he was. The Baggley family, who ran the Nottingham Road Nurseries, were especially fond of pilot Harry North who, as a fellow Methodist, would occasionally take service in the local chapels. The relationship was reciprocal: when the Nurseries ran short of water during a drought, a bowser came from the aerodrome, for the officers' mess feared for the Baggleys' tomatoes. The Methodist Chapel on the Green became a canteen, where airmen could go in the evening and often stay till late at night, playing billiards, eating home cooking and singing.

On 18 July 1942 there was a wedding at the Methodist Chapel when Ron Doubleday was married. Several airmen attended. The following night, 19/20 July, saw George Hawes and Bill Blair take off again in their Lancaster, and then again on the night of 21/22 July. This time the target was Duisburg. Again on the night of 23/24 they took off in their Lancaster, N for Nuts, again to raid Duisburg. The crew was Flt Sgt Hawes, pilot and captain from Australia, Flt Sgt Chiasson from Canada, Sgt Cartwright, Sgt Clarke and Sgt Smith of the RAF; Sgt Hooper from New Zealand, the 2nd pilot, and Flt Sgt Blair from Canada, who probably flew as rear gunner, although he was also a trained bomb-aimer. Bob Weatherall was due to go too, but his Lancaster had magneto trouble. The following morning he woke to find George and Bill had not returned. 'I was stunned by the news; it couldn't be. All my pals wiped out in one night'. This was George Hawes' 25th operation with 207 Squadron; his 'plane had been delivered new in June 1942 and had flown 17 operations. Bill Blair's body was washed ashore near Ijmuiden, Holland, on 12 October 1942. No other trace of 'plane or aircrew has ever been discovered.

It is difficult to appreciate today how the airmen, soldiers and Bottesford people coped with all this. 207 Squadron lost three 'planes in July 1942, five in August, three in September 1942 and so it went on. In September 1942, 207 Squadron went to Langar, and 467 RAAF Squadron took over in November. There followed a year's intensive flying from Bottesford with some extraordinary raids. Lancasters flew to Turin and Milan in Italy and then on to North Africa to re-fuel and return. On the Turin raid of 12/13 July 1943, one Lancaster crashed in Switzerland, one went missing and a third broke up in mid-air on the approach to the airfield.

In November 1943 the Americans arrived to make final preparations for the invasion of France. The 50th Troop Carrying Wing of the US IX Air Force came, with their Dakota troop-carrying aircraft. Several US units then passed through Bottesford, as part of the huge build-up towards D-Day. Training involved the development of two aspects — dropping men and supplies by parachute, and later, towing gliders. By the time of D-Day the build-up was complete, most units moving south. But several parachute and glider troops left from airfields in this vicinity direct to France. In particular, local people recall the gliders: one day the airfield was packed with them and the next they were all gone.

US troops spent a shorter time here than the airmen of the RAF and the soldiers of No 17 Petrol Depôt, but they made a considerable impression. Most of them went to Nottingham for entertainment so they were not such frequent visitors. There was a time of great tragedy when a lorry-load of US airmen was returning from a dance in Melton and several were killed. The lorry hit a tree on the corner at the beginning of Long Lane. The Americans are remembered with affection, especially by some of the younger people in the village whom they met in a social centre in Albert Street. The boys then living at Beechwood still remember Pfc Weinham of Ohio. The Americans were polite, they had good manners and, when they left, many wrote letters of thanks. Older villagers were worried by them but, between November 1943 and July 1944, Bottesford's integration into the internationally aware world of the 20th century moved a little faster.

The farming community worked extremely hard during the war, helped by the Women's Land Army and then by German and Italian prisoners, such as Signor Mario d'Agata, who stayed with Mr and Mrs Roberts. Fordson tractors were used to plough up land which had been pasture for centuries. The ground badly needed draining but there was neither the time nor the opportunity. The great strength of Bottesford was its self-sufficiency. George Hawes offered lessons in trapping and shooting rabbits learnt on the outback in Australia. He had come to the right place; rabbit became the staple diet. The Sutton family had a pigeon loft above their pig sty – both admirable sources of food. Licences to kill pigs and beasts were carefully controlled by the authorities, but no one could stop the trade in rabbit, both for meat and for their dressed skins which were turned into gloves. One essential service was provided by the Spick Brothers – that of collecting scrap iron and delivering it to the furnaces for war industry.

Bottesford had played its part to the full; the Petrol Depôt made a major contribution to the war effort, not least with an enormous build-up to D-Day, when so much petrol was required. Lt Moss moved south and was involved with PLUTO, the Pipe Line Under the Ocean which took petrol under the Channel. Yet, the success of the bomber campaign is still controversial. However, Rommel's son, Oberburgermeister Manfred Rommel, has recently written: 'it was after D-Day that the strength of the German armies flagged owing ultimately to the successive blows dealt by the American and British air forces to the supply of raw materials to the armaments industry and to the transport system of the 3rd Reich'. The village also paid the price of war; fifteen Bottesford men were killed and hundreds of men from 207 Squadron and 467 Squadron died. When the survivors returned in 1945 and 1946 they found an exhausted village, but one which had lived through the most extraordinary experiences.

Life in an English Hamlet, Normanton

It is situated in the corner of Leicestershire, one mile south of Lincolnshire, half a mile as the crow flies west is Nottinghamshire. It is a small hamlet. Up to the 19th century it was occupied by a community of farmers and farm-workers. There is no church, no shops, public house or any form of entertainment. As a lifetime resident born two years before the First World War, I will describe the way of life as it was seen by the residents up to the 1970s.

Very little in the way of improving the village took place until after the war of 1914–1918. The road from the neighbouring village of Bottesford was made up of large boulders of stone, suitable for the only transport available, horse and cart or on foot. Grass on the wide verge side of the road was let to farmers for cattle grazing by the Council. This work was called tenting. The winter nights were dreary. Snow was frequently known to be drifted well high over the hedge tops. Water frozen on the ponds to the thickness of three to four inches, which made sliding or skating one of the amusements for children. Their other sports was self made: Tin Lurkey, Fox and Hounds, Hide and Seek, Skipping, Marbles, Whip and Top or just walking in the fields. All sorts of English wildlife could be seen: foxes, hares, grass-snakes and also the known vermin, rats and mice. The bird life was abundant: pheasants, partridge, crows, wood-pigeon and the heron, and of the smaller type, wrens, robins, bullfinch, blackbirds and the thrush, also many more of the English variety. The wild flowers was there in all descriptions: buttercups, daisies, violets and scores more in hedgerows, coverts and spinneys. Mushrooms grew in abundance. Wells supplied the only drinking water available. Water troughs or tubs as they were so called caught the rainwater for the use by the housewife for washing and all manner of purposes. Utensils used were dolly-pegs, dolly-tubs, the all wooden roller mangle, the dishcloth for the pots, floor cloths, scrubbing brushes and soft soap for the floors, which were red and blue tiled. The firegrates were the old iron type, oven and boiler held together with bars to hold in the fire. Water was boiled on it, irons warmed on it and the roast was cooked by it. The boiler provided the hot water. Firewood sticks were collected from fields by mother and children. Coal was scarce but available by horse drawn cart from the nearest railway siding or railway station. The livelihood of the population was farming. Most requirements were self produced – potatoes, lettuce and all the well known varieties of vegetables. Poultry was kept for fresh eggs and the occasional meal of roast chicken. Rabbit meat and potato pie was a favourite mid-day meal. Two boiled eggs, fresh bread and farm butter and the housewife's fresh buttered scones provided a good afternoon tea. Each house had an outer shed known as a pig-sty, which housed a pig to eat the scraps and to provide the bacon for breakfast. Work commenced at daybreak and often ended on the farm late at night. Wages were around thirty shillings for a 48 hour week. Farm labourers' houses provided free for a few hours' work, often required on Sundays. Names changed very little in the way of new tenancy, everything seemed to keep the same. It was handed down from father to son. Rents paid by the farmers to the landlord, the Duke of Rutland. Rents were around 7s 6d an acre. Milk was delivered by one of the farmer's daughters to those in the village who required it, at 3d a pint. Bread was brought in an enclosed horse-drawn van by the baker from the village a mile or so away.

Something of a big change came around the 1920s, when the Duke decided to sell the village. Farms, farm houses and cottages, everything as the village stood: but with the great relief of worry to the tenant a choice to buy, at a reasonable valuation price of around £10 to £30 per acre (the farm), which was then in their occupation. The word mortgage was never or little heard of by village folk, but it soon became a word on everybody's lips. The slump was not long to follow. Changes came and went. Some not for the better. Corn prices were low, work became short, jobs hard to find. Farming changed from arable to grazing. Farm-hands changed jobs to work in the neighbouring lime pits or on the Great Northern railway nearby. Farmers then relied on family labour or with some form of casual help. Little seemed to change in the village then for a number of years except for the great Airship, the R 101, crossing over, when everybody turned out to see it pass but within weeks after, it crashed, a big disaster of its time. Now as the years passed little did the village people know the air ministry had a plan for an aerodrome, which was being proposed to be built on the land in the village. From then on great changes developed. A pill box was built in a field on the roadwide; a small attachment of soldiers arrived with searchlights and anti-aircraft guns. This soon put new life in the village. Children cycling up, also adults, to see these huge beams of light criss-crossing our skies at night, pinpointing small aircraft which looked like silver birds in the sky. Ministry letters were soon to follow to commandeer our land. Huge bulldozers, D.H. Scrapers and a vast quantity of equipment was brought almost on our doorstep. Roads were widened, corners straightened and an army of Irish navvies arrived. The name Wimpey could be seen everywhere. Large concrete runways were soon to be laid, hangars built. The first batch of American Dakota aircraft* was landing around us, towing gliders and all sorts of airforce equipment. By now we are on the map. The Yanks are here. Life in a big way has come to the village. Canteens for airmen and WAAFs, film shows and all sorts of entertainment, but we was to hear the bad news — War had been declared on Germany. The L.D.V. later known as the Home Guard had been formed. Gas masks supplied, ration books, air-raid shelters, everybody of military age had to register for service, but being of the farming community we were exempt. The sound of aircraft, army and airforce trucks bungling by, the black-out as it was so called, enforced by law, windows barricaded, the storm lamps shaded and car lamps dimmed, and every form of night light screened. Modern equipment was not available in the village. Electricity, tap water, telephones were some distance away. Water bowsers, electric generators supplied the forces. By now the Lancasters were here, replacing the Dakota aircraft.* Everything was a nightmare. Traffic moving in all directions, the sound the drone of heavy German bombers in the sky. The thud of bombs dropping in the distance. Our own aircraft limping home from the Rhine. The occasional ones crashing and bursting into flames in the field. Life in the village was of mixed feelings and fear. Gasmasks on the shoulder. The smell of gunpowder in the air but still the war dragged on. Food was by now one of the first priorities. The Government introduced subsidies. Grass was being turned under by the plough, corn was essential. Better prices were fixed. Horse meat was in great demand. Horses were leaving the farms in numbers. Dealers offering large prices everywhere. War Agricultural Committees under contract, doing the heavy work on the farms by tractor. Horse names Flower, Blossom and Duke were soon to be only a memory. The better things were to follow when peace was declared.

The village life then was soon to change. Farmers who had farmed in the villages a lifetime were preparing to retire. Farms changed hands, fresh breeds of cattle were seen, Friesian replacing the Lincoln Red, modern forms of breeding introduced, calves born by artificial insemination. Telephone and electric poles could be seen everywhere. The improvements of a modern age were with us. Tap water and sewers, television — a new form of entertainment — combined harvesters, tractors, balers, driers and trailers, all modern equipment. Horse drawn implements rotting under the hedges. All forms of sprays were introduced, rabbits were dying of myxomatosis, ponds filled in, cowslips and wild orchids, dandelions and thistles and many more variety of flowers almsot extinct. Frogs and tadpoles were a thing of the past. Intensive farming, battery hens, pigs crated and tethered, cows de-horned. New medicines or treatments to cattle, calcium for milk fever, cottages occupied by townfolk, hangers on the airfield used for storage, runways deteriorating, a reminder of the past. But still life goes on in our small hamlet, but:

Now here is my story ending,
I'll finish it off in rhyme:
We are still in the 1900s
The year is '79
It is a life that I remember
With little for me to boast
To this very last year's that past us
Its awakened the Normanton ghost.

W. Robinson

* The American Dakota planes arrived in 1943, after the airfield had been in use for two years.

Verses on Normanton

Now here is a little story
Or shall we say a rhyme
It's about a little hamlet
That's been here for some time.

An aerodrome was built here
With many stories one can tell
There were billets there for airmen
Near to Thaxon's Well.

The WAAFs we know were jolly
I well remember still
They had their sleeping quarters
On Little Folly Hill.

The Lancaster bombers
Based here upon this very 'drome
Were sent on bombing missions
To Germany or to Rome.

Now these brave airmen
In Bottesford churchyard lay
A memory that is with us
To this very day.

Bottesford Aerodrome. (BBH)

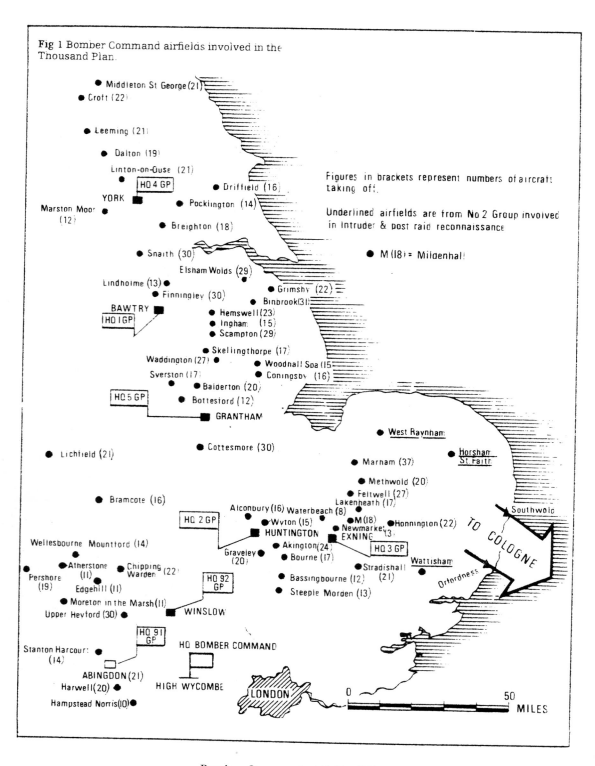

Fig 1 Bomber Command airfields involved in the Thousand Plan.

Figures in brackets represent numbers of aircraft taking off.

Underlined airfields are from No 2 Group involved in Intruder & post raid reconnaissance

M (18) = Mildenhall

● Middleton St George (21)
● Croft (22)
● Leeming (21)
● Dalton (19)
Linton-on-Ouse (21)
HQ 4 GP
YORK
● Driffield (16)
● Pocklington (14)
Marston Moor (12)
● Breighton (18)
● Snaith (30)
Elsham Wolds (29)
Lindholme (13)
● Finningley (30)
● Grimsby (22)
BAWTRY
HQ 1 GP
● Binbrook(31)
● Hemswell (23)
● Ingham (15)
● Scampton (29)
● Skellingthorpe (17)
Waddington (27)
● Woodhall Spa (15)
Syerston (17)
● Coningsby (16)
● Balderton (20)
HQ 5 GP
● Bottesford (12)
GRANTHAM
● West Raynham
● Cottesmore (30)
● Lichfield (21)
● Marham (37)
● Horsham St Faith
● Methwold (20)
● Feltwell (27)
● Bramcote (16)
Lakenheath (17)
Alconbury (16) Waterbeach (8)
HQ 2 GP
● Wyton (15) ● M (18)
● Honnington (22)
HUNTINGTON
Newmarket (3)
EXNING
TO COLOGNE
Southwold
Wellesbourne Mountford (14)
Graveley (20)
Akington(24)
HQ 3 GP
● Stradishall (21)
Wattisham
● Atherstone (11)
● Chipping Warden (22)
● Bourne (17)
Orfordness
Pershore (19)
Edgehill (11)
● Bassingbourne (12)
HQ 92 GP
● Moreton in the Marsh(11)
● Steeple Morden (13)
Upper Heyford (30)
WINSLOW
HQ 91 GP
HQ BOMBER COMMAND
Stanton Harcourt (14)
ABINGDON(21)
Harwell(20)
HIGH WYCOMBE
LONDON
Hampstead Norris(10)
0   50 MILES

Bomber Command airfields 1942.

124

ABOVE: Flt Sgt Atkinson's Manchester bomber crew 1942 — George Hawes back left, Bill Blair front right. (JS) BELOW: Flt Sgt Hawes holding the propellor of his Lancaster bomber. (JS)

ABOVE: A Manchester in the snow at Bottesford. (207) LEFT: Flt Sgt
Bill Blair's grave in Amsterdam. BELOW: Commonwealth War Graves
at Amsterdam Cemetery.

R.75117 FLIGHT SERGEANT
T.C. BLAIR
AIR GUNNER
ROYAL CANADIAN AIR FORCE
24TH JULY 1942   AGE 33

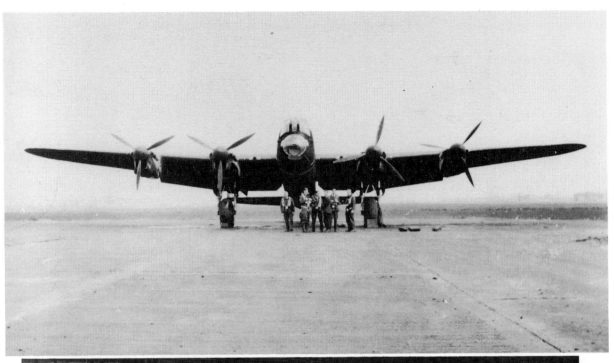

ABOVE: A Lancaster with crew. (207) BELOW: Air crew graves in
Bottesford cemetery.

ABOVE: The airfield in 1989. (HER) RIGHT: The signal box, hit in the 1941 raid. BELOW: The Army camp in 1989.

ABOVE: Signor Mario d'Agata — Italian POW, RIGHT: Charles Spick
and BELOW: Robin Spick in 1989.

129

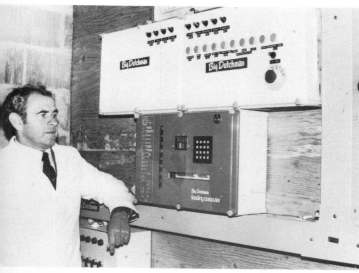

RIGHT: Daniel Daybell contemplates the changing world of Bottesford c1910. ABOVE: The Victory Commemoration Hall. (HER) CENTRE: Ken Greasley and his computerised cattle feed. (AJ) BELOW: St Mary's Choir, 1949.

A Changing Community

After the Second World War farmers and their sons naturally tended to think in terms of milk; after all, this concentration on dairy cattle rather than arable had been the vogue before the disruption. Initially, older farmers remembered the drift back to pasture following the First World War and the Duke's sale in 1920. But the circumstances of 1945 were different. The Government was determined above all else to keep import bills down to maximise income from exports – the slogan *export or die* became the watchword of Labour. Alongside this economic policy lay the Government's social policies: the determination to improve the nation's health led to an ever-increasing concentration on milk. Bottesford farmers were now in an enviable position. An Act of 1947 covered about three quarters of farming produce, using guaranteed prices and deficiency payments to subsidise home produced food, and to offset the competition from foreign agriculture. Mixed farming came into its own, and mechanisation, especially using the ubiquitous Ferguson tractor, enabled local farmers to extend cereal production. Thus started, the trend to cereals, backed by dairy farming, developed among the farmers whose land lay on the outskirts of the village. Those farmers, especially Mr Len Palmer, who lived close to the railway line, developed milk and milk bottling plants. The use of tractors proved valuable in another case when Mr George Upton of Beckingthorpe Farm ploughed up a perfect 1860 gold sovereign in September 1950!

The tractor was established in Bottesford during the Second World War and thereafter mechanisation developed apace. For a while in the 1940s and the 1950s dairying kept ahead of arable, but increasingly stringent hygiene regulations, especially the insistence upon pasteurisation, forced local farmers to give up their milk rounds. Mr Palmer gradually built up a herd of Friesians from his pre-war mixed herd of Lincoln Red, Shorthorns and Friesians. Dairy farming proved labour intensive and it was rare for farmers and their dairymen to take holidays. This proved a major factor in the gradual shift away from dairying, first to concentrate on stock breeding and fattening, which was becoming more profitable in the 1960s, and then to concentrate on arable and sheep, which is the style today.

We have witnessed a total reversal of farming in Bottesford. In 1066 the concentration was on cereals, with virtually the whole parish ploughed up. Gradually sheep were added, by around 1300, to bring about a small, piecemeal enclosure, largely in the central area of the Parish. Then in the 16th and 17th centuries sheep were widespread, cereals were still important and clover leys began to be sown, which brought about a development in cattle grazing for fattening. Gradually the majority of the Parish became pasture, with a concentration on fatstock in the early 19th century. With the development of the railway, the slowly growing Stilton cheese dairy herds were diversified to produce milk for town consumption, leading to dairy farming's dominance in the early 20th century. In the second half of the century, Government subsidies and common market quotas have brought about a shift from dairying, which is hardly carried out at all in the village today, to fattening beasts to some degree, and to the major concentration on oil seed rape and wheat which dominates Parish fields. The understandable unwillingness of farm workers to work seven days a week and 365 days a year, to milk twice a day, is one factor in the reversion to arable farming. Now the village fields look similar to how they must have looked 900 years ago; the difference would be the vast quantity of weeds in the fields of the past, now done away with by chemical fertilisers and the modern short stalked wheat, brought about by the end of demand for long straw for thatching and the development of short-straw varieties to suit the demands of combining.

These changes are all the more dramatic when the reality of village life in the immediate years post-war is remembered. Bottesford still boasts of being the last place attacked by an enemy plane on 20 March 1945: the red light on the church tower was not removed until August 1951. Until 1947, village schoolchildren left the all-through elementary school opposite the Cross and Stocks at the age of 14. There was no TV service during the 1940s, and there was still no piped water; the Parish Council were looking after village pumps in Easthorpe and Normanton. There was no mains sewerage – the Rural District Council emptied the cesspits weekly. Milk was delivered twice daily by the local farmers, chiefly Mr and Mrs Cyril Palmer from Church Farm. Street lighting was the responsibility of the Parish Council. Allotments too were a major responsibility of the Parish Council, and taken seriously. The village had gas and electricity. Property prices had not yet started to rocket: the baker's house in Chapel Street was sold for £1,075 in 1947. The Rutland Arms was sold for £16,000 in 1950, when four cottages in Easthorpe went for £500. However, the village Friendly Society was wound up and rents were tightly controlled – the old Mill House in Queen Street had its rent reduced in 1950 to the 1914 level of £16 per annum.

The story of the development of the village since the Second World War is one firstly of the relocation of military huts, then of the installation of water and sewerage, and finally of an enormous house-building programme. There were old huts to be disposed of from the Army camp and the airfield. Mr Norris in the High Street still uses his hut from the Army camp in 1989, but most of the temporary accommodation has gone. The WI which started in 1926 had donated its original hut to the village, and this became the nucleus of the long-planned village hall, the Victory Commemoration Hall. A playing field off Belvoir Road was purchased and the Football Club was able to move; originally it played in the field immediately north-west of the Normanton level crossing.

Water mains were laid and at long last tap water came, in 1951. Most village houses have since then filled in their wells and dismantled the pumps, but those few which remain are invaluable in summer time. With mains water it became realistic to extend the housing stock. This was done partly by local council initiatives, partly by private builders within the village, and partly by big estate developments. Pre-war council houses were supplemented in the 1950s by an extensive estate, with Silverwood Road, named after the Post Office family and Keel Drive, named after a chairman of the Parish Council. The Rural District Council decided to concentrate housing for older people in Bottesford, and several bungalows, maisonettes and flats were built, especially the Warwick Flats, with good communal accommodation. This housing by the local Council was extended along the High Street when the old Hand's Charity houses were taken down and replaced by four new bungalows. These were occupied by old people from the 19th century Redford Cottages, off Chapel Street, which were then pulled down.

The builder of most of these houses was Mr W.J. Roberts, who gradually built up an extensive Bottesford concern. As more and more building became possible in the improving economic climate of the 1950s Mr Roberts undertook several local projects. He built the council houses, several private houses and his own workshops in Barkestone Lane. Many cottages were pulled down during the fifties, a policy entirely in accord with local government policy to remove old housing, rather than renovate it, as now prevails. Mr Roberts became the biggest employer and new employment patterns emerged. In the 19th century, agricultural labourers had dominated the village: in the latter 20th century the great employers of labour are no longer the farmers, but builders like Mr Roberts and, latterly, Mr K. Greasley. Mechanisation of farming has reinforced this change: skilled workers turn now to bricklaying, carpentering, plastering, painting, roofing, electrical installation and plumbing. Such diversification has come about naturally and today many working people are self-employed – a big change from the agricultural labourer in his tied cottage.

The largest locally built building was Mr Roberts' Belvoir High School. The village profited considerably from the Leicestershire County Council's progressive education policy. The all-age school in the village centre, dangerously sited on the A52, was half emptied in 1958 by the construction of a secondary modern school off Barkestone Lane. This building has stood the test of time – now over 30 years old, it is a tribute to local craftsmanship. The school became a 10-14 year age range High School in 1968 and has been extended into a community centre with the addition of a sports hall, named after Mr L.S. Dewey, the first headmaster of the secondary school. Its building was jointly funded by the local community and the County Council. In 1977 an attractive primary school for the 5-10 age range was built next to the High School. The educational campus has now been completed by the construction by self-help of the Bottesford Play Group building. The Playgroup first opened in 1967 and was able to open its own premises 21 years later.

It was Mr Roberts' firm which installed the sewerage system in 1961. This proved a complex job, as running sands just under the topsoil made digging tunnels expensive. But once the village had effective drainage, new estates could be built. First the West End estate was developed in the 1960s, then the Beckingthorpe estate in the 1970s. On the latter estate W. Davis and Co, a Leicester building firm, built a pair of semi-detached houses in less than a fortnight, to prove just how quickly a good, modern, brick house could be constructed. During the 1980s the village has expanded even more, with big estates off Barkestone Lane and between Albert Street and Pinfold Lane.

During the 1960s, '70s and '80s population has expanded and often the carefully considered plans of local councils have been overtaken by events. The County Plan at the beginning of the 1980s stated that planning consent would not normally be granted for more than 150 dwellings between 1981 and 1996. In fact there were 186 completions between 1981 and 1988. The latest policy statement by Melton Borough Council, January 1989, gives a total of 959 dwellings in Bottesford, of which 186 have been built since 1981. 124 of the grand total were Council-owned properties in September 1988; the oldest are now undergoing a total renovation. All this building is essential to house a population which has altered dramatically. The following figures have been worked out by the Melton Borough Council for the area of Bottesford village alone:

1974	1975	1976	1977	1978	1979	1980	1981	1982	1983	1984	1985	1986	1987
1840	1933	1997	2061	1064	2104	2124	2170	2182	2193	2143	2174	2244	2345

This rate of expansion is similar to that of the early part of the 19th century. That was accompanied by a great rebuilding – so too has this latest development.

Farming continues to be a major activity, with the 10th Duke of Rutland still owning much land. The Hospital Farm, Muston, has around ⅓ pasture and ⅔ arable land. It is one of a group of farms tenanted by the Donger family, who have successfully farmed in Muston and Bottesford throughout this century. In Bottesford one of the major families of the village today are the Norrises: one branch farms extensively, partly on the Duke's land, and partly on their own. Mr Aubrey Norris and his sons have also diversified, owning transport and earth-moving vehicles. The Taylor family farms extensively too, with three farms and one of the village's three butchery shops, still owning their own slaughterhouse. The different branches of the Goodson family farm and have a butcher's shop, and the village's third butcher's shop is still owned by the George family. The Marsh family still farms in the village, with George Marsh's granddaughter at Beckingthorpe Farm.

This continuity of tenure reflects the last 1,000 years of farming in Bottesford. The village has absorbed such a population influx and the rebuilding of the last 30 years because it has retained the independent nature of its inhabitants. The stability of the community is clear from the way names stubbornly stay associated with places. The Wheatsheaf Inn in Muston has been nicknamed the Gap since before the 1770s. Palmer's Hill is still the local name of Beacon Hill, even though the Palmers left the farm some years ago. Granary Lane still connects Easthorpe Road with the playing field, although there is no granary in sight today. The old Coffee House of 1881 became a youth club in 1958 and this still maintains, in the centre of the village, a community meeting place. When it was badly damaged by fire in 1983, the rebuilding was supported by a great range of village organisations. Bottesford may have grown, and it may look different, but beneath its blue tiles and golden fields, it remains a country community, with its roots deep in its fertile soils.

ABOVE: The Officers' Mess of the Army Camp in 1989, and BELOW: one of the Army Camp huts, moved to the back of Mr Norris's house in High Street.

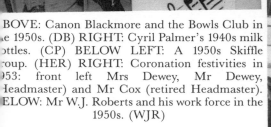

ABOVE: Canon Blackmore and the Bowls Club in the 1950s. (DB) RIGHT: Cyril Palmer's 1940s milk bottles. (CP) BELOW LEFT: A 1950s Skiffle Group. (HER) RIGHT: Coronation festivities in 1953: front left Mrs Dewey, Mr Dewey, (Headmaster) and Mr Cox (retired Headmaster). BELOW: Mr W.J. Roberts and his work force in the 1950s. (WJR)

LEFT: Ray Foster, butcher-boy for Millers in 1956. (HER) RIGHT: Jane Daybell with fox, 1956. (HER) BELOW: Mr W.J. Roberts installs the sewerage 1961. (WJR)

ABOVE LEFT: Cottages in Queen Street, now demolished. (HER) RIGHT: Singleton's house in Chapel Street just before it was pulled down in 1955. (HER) CENTRE LEFT: Mrs Lane with her Guides in 1960. (HER) RIGHT: The rebuilding of the Rectory by Mr K. Greasley, 1989. BELOW LEFT: Mr John Ball, roofing contractor. RIGHT: The Rector and the Scouts c1982. (IK)

ABOVE: LEFT TO RIGHT: Mr Ian Kitchener's shop, Mr Aubrey Norris, farmer, and transport contractor. (BH) Dr Morgan at Easthorpe Manor; CENTRE: Mr Philip Marsh, son of Mr George Marsh, Mr E.A. Shipman, Bradwell's Printers in the Army camp in 1989. BELOW: Belvoir High School. (WJR)

ABOVE LEFT: Modernisation of the Pinfold Lane council houses built
in the 1930s. (BH) RIGHT: The Chip Shop built by Mr Ken Greasley.
(BH) CENTRE LEFT: Mr W.J. Roberts and huntsman at the Meet of
the Belvoir Hunt, 1989. (HER) RIGHT: The village policeman 1989.
BELOW: Young people at the village ford in 1989.

ABOVE: The by-pass viewed from a micro-light by Mr G. Norris.
(HER) BELOW: Tranquil Bottesford, 1989.

Bibliography

General
Becket, J.V., *The East Midlands from AD 1000,* 1988
Brown, A., *Fieldwork for Archaeologists and Local Historians,* 1987
Dewey, L.S., *The North East Corner,* Belvoir High School, 1969
Esdaile, A., *Rutland Monuments,* 1845
Honeybone, M., *The Vale of Belvoir,* 1987
Hoskins, W.G., *Essays in Leicestershire History,* 1950
Levine, D., *Family Formation in an Age of Nascent Capitalism,* 1977
Macfarlane, A., *The Origins of English Individualism,* 1978
May, T., *An Economic and Social History of Britain,* 1987
Nichols, J., *The History and Antiquities of the County of Leicester, Vol. 2, part 1,* 1795
Rackham, O., *The History of the Countryside,* 1986
Richardson, J., *The Local Historians Encyclopedia,* 1986
V.C.H., *The Victoria County History — Leicestershire — 20th Century.*

Beautiful Bottesford
Bain, R.K., *Antique Maps of Leicestershire,* 1972
Ekwall, E., *English Place Names,* 1974
Gelling, M., *Place Names in the Landscape,* 1984
Hartley, R.F., *The Medieval Earthworks of N.E. Leicestershire,* 1987
Liddle, P., *Leicestershire Archaeology Vol. 1,* 1982
Liddle, P., *Leicestershire Archaeology Vol. 2,* 1982
Pickering, J. & Hartley, R.F., *Past Worlds in a Landscape,* 1983
Rowley, T., *Villages in the Landscape,* 1987

The Landowners
Fox Davies, A.C., *A Complete Guide to Heraldry,* 1985
Farnham, G.E., *Medieval Leicestershire Village Notes,* 1930s
H.M.C., *Manuscripts of His Grace the Duke of Rutland Vols I-IV,* 1888-1905
Mills, D.R., *Landownership and Rural Population in Leicestershire in the mid-19th Century,* Ph.D. 1963
Morgan, P. (ed), *Domesday Book Vol. 22 — Leicestershire,* 1979
Phythian-Adam, C. (ed), *The Norman Conquest of Leicestershire and Rutland,* 1986
Round, J.H., *The Origin of Belvoir Castle,* E.H.R. Vol. 22

Farmers and Tenants
Bruyn Andrews, C. (ed), *The Torrington Diaries,* 1935
Field, J., *English Field Names — a Dictionary,* 1989
Hoskins, W.G., *The Midland Peasant,* 1957
Hamilton Thompson, A., *Wyggeston Hospital Charters,* 1930s
Lyth, Philip, *A History of Nottinghamshire Farming,* 1989
Pitt, W.A., *A General View of the Agriculture of the County of Leicester,* 1809
Taylor, C., *Fields in the English Landscape,* 1987

Day Labour
Blacknor, J., *History of Nottingham,* 1815
David and Charles (pub.), *The First Edition of the Ordnance Survey Sleaford Sheet* — surveyed in the 19th century
King, W., *Map of Leicestershire, Lincolnshire and Nottinghamshire: a tract of country around Belvoir Castle,* 1806
Prior, J., *Map of Leicestershire,* 1777
Lowe, D. & Richards, J., *The Lace Heritage,* 1984
Lowe, D. & Richards, J., *The City of Lace,* 1983
Wilson, Catherine, *A Checklist of Windmill Printing by Karl Wood* L.C.C., 1982

Road versus Rail
Bottesford Community Centre, *The Belvoir Country News,* 1979
Cosson, H., *Turnpike Roads of Nottinghamshire,* 1934
Franks, D.L., *The Great Northern and London and North Western Junction Railway (GNLNWJR),* 1974
Hadfield, C., *British Canals,* 1963
Hadfield, C., *The Canals of the East Midlands,* 1970
Honeybone, M., *The Book of Grantham,* 1988
Honeybone, M., *The Vale of Belvoir,* 1987
Howard Anderson, P., *Forgotten Railways Vol. 2 — The East Midlands,* 1985
Jervoise, E., *Ancient Bridges of Mid and Eastern England,* 1932
Leleux, R., *The East Midlands — Vol. 9 of a Regional History of the Railways of Great Britain,* 1976
Philpotts, R., *The Grantham Canal Early Days,* 1976
Shipman, E.A. (ed), *The Cross and Stocks — a Bottesford magazine,* 1968-9

Bricks, Blessings and Bread
Ashby, Jane, E., *English Medieval Murals of the Doom,* M.Phil York 1980
Brown, R.J., *The English Country Cottage,* 1984
Brown, R.J., *English Farmhouse,* 1985
Brimskill, R.W., *Traditional Buildings of Britain,* 1988
Mercer, E., *English Vernacular Houses* RCHM, 1975
Pevsner, N., *Buildings of England — Leicestershire and Rutland* 2nd Ed. by Elizabeth Williamson, 1984
R.C.H.M. England, *Nonconformist Chapels and Meeting Houses in Leicestershire, Nottinghamshire and Rutland,* 1986
Shipman, E.A., *The Church of St. Mary the Virgin, Bottesford,* 1982
Thompson, D.M., *Church and Society in Leicestershire,* Ph.D. 1969
Woodforde, J., *Farm Buildings,* 1985

To Help One Another
Cocking, T., *A History of Wesleyan Methodism in Grantham,* 1836
Curtis, (ed), *Topographical History of Leicestershire,* 1820
Grantham Journal, *Grantham Journal* 1854 to present day
Kelly (ed) *Directory of Leicestershire and Rutland* 19th Century & 20th Century
Melville (ed), *County of Leicestershire Directory,* 1854
Post Office (ed), *Leicestershire County Directories,* 19th Century & 20th Century
White (ed), *Leicestershire County Directories,* 19th Century & 20th Century
Wright, *Leicestershire County Directory,* 1894

The Duke's Sale
Collett, V.C., and Whitehead, J., *How to spend a holiday in the Vale of Belvoir,* about 1903
Escritt & Barrell, *Part of the Belvoir Estate — Sale Catalogue,* 1920
Escritt & Barrell, *Sale Catalogue — Church Lands, Bottesford,* 1920
Harrison, W.G. (ed), *Guide to Belvoir, Bottesford and District,* 1922
Tuxford, Miss H.H., *Cookery for the Middle Classes,* 1926

The Impact of War
Ian Allen Ltd. (ed), *The R.A.F. Handbook 1939-1945,* 1987
Halley, J.J., *The Squadrons of the R.A.F.,* 1980
Halpenny, B.B., *Action Stations 2*
Matanle, I., *World War II,* 1989
Middlebrook, M. & Everitt, C., *The Bomber Command Diaries,* 1985
Rope, Denise, *For the Duration — Diaries and Letters Home of Flt Sgt W.G. Hawes,* 1984

A Changing Community
Bottesford Community Centre, *Belvoir Country News,* 1979
Melton Borough Council, *Bottesford: a draft interim policy statement,* 1989
Newark Advertiser, Saturday, January 18th — Article, 1975

Index

Figures in italics refer to illustrations

Key to Caption Credits

207	207 Squadron RAF collections
AE	Andrew Esdaile *Rutland Monuments* (1845)
B	Mrs Bond's collection
BBH	Bruce B. Halfpenny *Action Stations*
BPCC	Bottesford Parochial Church Council
CC	Mr and Mrs Crabtree's collection
CP	Mr and Mrs Cyril Palmer's collection
DB	Mrs Dorothy Beedham's collection
DF	Daybell family collection
DL	David Levine *Family Formation in an Age of Nascent Capitalism* (1979)
EAS	Mr E.A. Shipman
EJ	E. Jervoise *Ancient Bridges in Mid and Eastern England*
GC	Rev George Cooper
HER	Mr H.E. Rayson
IK	Mr Ian Kitchener's collection – Scout photographs
JC	Mrs Jackson's collection
JN	John Nichols *History and Antiquities of the County of Leicester Vol II part I* (1790s)
JS	Mrs Joyce Smith's collection
LCC	Lincs. County Council Recreational Services – Usher Art Gallery
LRO	Leicestershire Record Office
LTD	Lord Torrington's *Diaries*
NEC	Mr L.S. Dewey *The North East Corner*
NRO	Nottinghamshire Record Office
PM	Mrs Pam Millership's collection
R	Mrs Reed's collection
RC	Rev R. Cleland, Master of Wyggeston Hospital, Leicester
RFH	R.F. Hartley *Medieval Earthworks of NE Leicestershire* (1988)
SM	Mrs S. Meech's collection
VC	Victor Collett *How to Spend a Holiday in the Vale of Belvoir* (1902)
VPE	Mr Vaughan Evans
WJR	Mr and Mrs W.J. Roberts' collection

Subscribers

Presentation Copies

1 Bottesford Parish Council
2 Melton Borough Council
3 Leicestershire County Council
4 Leicestershire County Library Service, Bottesford Branch
5 Leicestershire Records Office
6 His Grace The Duke of Rutland
7 Alan Reed
8 Rev Kenneth Dyke

9 Michael & Diana Honeybone
10 Clive & Carolyn Birch
11 Molly Ford
12 Mr & Mrs N.R. Carter
13 R. A. Boyce
14 T. Noon
15 Mrs P. Hallam
16 Dennis Bentley
17 Mrs Margaret Cook
18 Mrs H.N.J. Allen
19 Mr & Mrs I.H. Davies
20 R.H. Hulse
21 Mr & Mrs A.M. Dixon
22 Mr & Mrs W.P. Maxwell
23 Mr & Mrs T.W. Reason
24 Mrs I.G. Bellamy
25 Brett Clifford
26 Bobby Donger
27 Mrs E. Gunnell
28 Mr & Mrs R. Garrett
29 Mrs E. Hodson
30 P. D. Wilson
31 Mrs E. Daybell
32 Mr & Mrs A. Millership
33 David Booth
34 Gina Topps
35 S.J. Galpin
36 Jane Moulton
37 Mr & Mrs Cyril Palmer
38 Mr & Mrs G. Pedge
39 Mrs Sue Arnold
40 Mrs G.R. Norris
41 Mr & Mrs Richard H. Donger
42 Mr & Mrs C.W. Donger
43 Mr & Mrs W.R. Barke
44 Mrs J. Bagnall
45 Mrs I. Harty
46 Canon C.J.R. Daybell
47 E.A. Shipman
48 P.J. Summerfield
49 Mrs Ivy McElroy
50 Helen McElroy
51 Shelley Phillips
52 Audrey Bushell
53 Mr & Mrs W. Cain
54 Mrs Ena Lane
55 John Lane
56 Howard Power
57 Richard Greenhough

58 Humphrey Lingard
59 Miss Margaret Taylor
60 Mrs M. Clarke
61 A. Munro
62 P.M. Gudgeon
63 Peter & Peggy Topps
64 David & Julian Jones
65 T.W. Marsh
66 Mr & Mrs Feary
67 G.N. Crabtree
68 John & Jean Hammond
69 Margaret Drew
70 Mr & Mrs Bates
71 Mr & Mrs Dennis Kirk
72 Brian Cooper
73 Mrs Evelyn Jallands
74 Mrs Andrew Goodson
75 Helen M. Boyd
76 John David Brown
77 David Boyd
78 A.E. Welsh
79 Mrs Mary Chapman
80 Geoffrey Sentance
81 Dorothy Beedham
82 T. Brewster
83 J.R. Brewster
84 P.A. Brewster
85 J.C. Brewster
86 Mrs Mavis Minkley
87 Hugh Watson
88 Miss Susan Watkins
89 Mrs F. Dunwell
90 Gloria Shawcroft
91 Chris Ashworth
92 Mrs Jackson
93 Colin & Susan Love
94 Mr & Mrs Lister
95 D.J. MacDonald
96 Rev K. Dyke

97 Bottesford Parochial Church Council
98 Rev G.J. Cooper
99 Gerald Norris
100 G.C. Clack
101 Mrs J. Taylor
102 Mrs Jean Round
103 Mrs O. Ball
104 Christopher Marston
105 Karen Marston
106 David Cain
107 D.A. Rayson
108 T. Rayson
109 Mrs Hogan
110 Mr & Mrs Richard Taylor
111 Edward & Marion Flitney
112 J. & D. Flintham
113 Mr & Mrs A.B. Davies
114 Jane Walton
115 I. & J. Harra
116 J. & K. Harra
117 Baughan Evans
118 Mr & Mrs D.A.T. Cooper
119 Mrs F.W. Evans
120 Mr F.W. Harrison
121 Herr u Frau Kiener
122 Mr & Mrs D. Andrews
123 Mrs Gladys Marston
124 Mrs Janet Dammes
125 Malcolm & Mary Owen
126 Miss M.W. Slight
127 Kesteven & Grantham Girls School
128 Miss J. Whicker
129 Dorothy Tasney
130 Marjorie Hawley
131 Frederick T. Musson

132 Mrs Jeanne Gilbert
133 W.A. Ablewhite
134 Mrs P. Baggaley
135 Mrs Joyce Smith
136 Dudley Reeves
137 S. Cain
138 Miss Elizabeth Burrows
139 Mr J. Moulsher
140 John Ball
141 Terry Box
142 Mr & Mrs W.J. Burrows
143 The Blair Family, Canada
144 The Hawes Family, Australia
145 Mr & Mrs Hornby
146 Mr & Mrs H.C. Honeybone
147 Mr & Mrs M.J.S. Bayley
148 Mr & Mrs J.A. Honeybone
149 Prof & Mrs R.C. Honeybone
150 Mr & Mrs G.J. Gilbody
151 Mr & Mrs M. Knapp
152 Mr & Mrs David Gray
153 Mrs S.A. Pitman
154 Miss Alice Trickett
155 Mrs Freda Farrand
156 Ben Honeybone
157 Mrs G. Rhodes
158 David Kaye
159 Alison Honeybone
160 Patrick Honeybone
161 Miss Jean Liddell
162 Mr & Mrs S.D. Owen
163 Michael Taylor
164 Mrs Jane Barrington-Fuller
165 Mr & Mrs H. Blower
166 Dr Sara Blower
167 J.A. Panter
168 Philip Marsh
169 Mrs O. Sutherland
170 H.S. Johnson
171 Dr N.K. Woll
172 H.N. Carolan
173 N.H. Parnham
174 R.A.M. Welsh
175 Jennifer Dyer
176 John Marcus Hamer
177 K. Kirton
178 Terence Pizzey
179 John Goodson
180 W.A. Woodthorpe
181 Mr & Mrs G. Burrows

182	R.H. Rawson	230	Alastair & Carole Crooke
183	Mr & Mrs Dickson	231	Jan & Alf Williams
184	Mrs Joanne Silverwood	232	Peter & Kath Marriott
185	Mr Kilner	233	Mr & Mrs L. Watson
186	Robert Evans	234	Isobel Spencer
187	J. Goodman	235	Gary & Collette Brown
188	Alan Jackson	236	Mr & Mrs J. Price
189	B. Turton	237	Neville Spick
190	Sue Dunsmore	238	V.A. Money
191	Jill Squire	239	Mrs M. Carr
192	F. Wilkinson	240	Mrs S.A. Pitman
193	Mrs S. Calcraft	241	Mrs Marshall
194	Irene Senescall	242	S. Southwell
195	Mr & Mrs Richard Epton	243	R. Charlton
196	Mrs A.C. Swindell	244	Mrs N. Charlton
197	Robert Taylor	245	Mrs S.M. Robertson
198	John Baggaley	246	Susan Heech
199	Miss Brenda Pask	247	B. Smith
200	John D. Ives	248	J. Clay
201	Mary Hamby	249	Mrs M.E. Marshall
202	Michael Kay	250	Mrs M. Seddon
203	Robin Spick	251	Mrs J. Spendlove
204	Mr & Mrs R.N. Priestland	252	W. Allen
205	Dr & Mrs R.L.W. Atkins	253	Jonathan Taylor
206	Mr & Mrs L.S. Hall	254	R.T. Bond
207	Mr & Mrs D. Cotterall	255	Mrs G. Claricoats
208	Canon W.N. Metcalfe	256	J. Peek
209	Bottesford Primary School	257	Mr & Mrs T. Marriott
210	207 Squadron RAF Association	258	Mrs J.A. Jepson
211	Lisa Pacey	259	Mrs Sayers
212	Mrs B. Wilbraham	260	Alan W. Reed
213	Mr & Mrs J. McCullough	261	Mrs S. Middleton
214	Mr & Mrs R.F. Jackson	262	Belvoir High School
215	Janet Lucas	263	Mr & Mrs W.J. Roberts
216	Mrs B. Scothorne	268	
217	Mr & Mrs B. Milnes	269	Ken Greasley
218	J.G. Raybould	278	
219	Mr & Mrs F.K.G. Moxon	279	Mrs J.M. Allsop
220	Janet & Paul Willcock	280	D.J. Walden
221	Mr & Mrs E.F. Edwards	281	G.N. Sharp
222	Mr & Mrs E. George	282	Mrs M. Dunn
223	Mr & Mrs V. Martin	283	Mrs C. Bolland
224	Harold Speed	284	Mrs H.M. Shephard
225	Mr & Mrs P.J. & J. Gledding	285	John McCarthy
226	Mr & Mrs D.P. Storer	286	W.T. Leonard
227	Mr & Mrs T.W. Fisher	287	
228	Mr & Mrs M.W. Kilby	288	Alan V. Rayson
229	Mr & Mrs C.F. Glover	289	Chris Spalding
		290	M.G. Morgan
		291	C.W. George
		292	Mrs E. Guy
		293	Stuart Colledge
		294	S.L. Berryman
		295	Karen & Paul Butcher
		296	Sibthorp Library
		297	Rex Robinson
		298	Nicholas Metcalfe
		299	
		300	T. Basil Hodgkinson
		301	Leicestershire

315	Libraries & Information Service	381	Mrs K. Ballinger
316	Lincolnshire	382	Nottinghamshire County Council
325	Library Service	387	
326	Mary E. Bland	388	Geoff Goode
327	John Clegg	389	Miss M.W. Slight
328	John Edward Ronan	390	D.S. Parker
329	A.M. & J.A. Bromell	391	S.N.M. Fisher
330	Mrs Pauline M. Prowett	392	Angela Baldwin
331	Craig Blackwell	393	Miss Margaret Cater
332	S.P. Parker	394	M.G. Hemming
333	Graham Victor Adams	395	Mrs Dawn Carlile
334	Mr & Mrs P.J. Finch	397	
335	Helen Miller	398	I.E. Ormesher
336	Sean F. Fenner	399	Peter Harris
337	Michael John Booth	400	H. Russell
338	Patrick M. Harris	401	David Carter
339	P.A. Foster	402	Ian Paul Smith
340	L.H. Thwaites	403	S.B. Barratt
341	W.H. Wiseman	404	P.J. & K.J. Morgan
342	Mrs L. Mitchell	405	Yvonne & David Cockayne
343	Brian Ingledew	406	Emily Cockayne
344	Sheila Murphy	407	R. Colchester
345	Mrs V. Robinson	408	R.A. Smith
346		409	Angela Kapellar
347	Graham Storrie	410	Claire Kapellar
348	Nicola J. Metcalfe	411	Mrs E.M. Fisher
349	A.H. Nevitte	412	G. Elms
350	N.S. Smith	413	Mrs I. Madell
351	Mrs E.M. Donger	414	K.R. Sells
352	Ruth Hotchin	415	Heather Bond
353	Mrs Rita Durant	416	
354	Mr & Mrs B. Silverwood	417	Mrs J.R. Morley
355	Lynne Potter	418	Mrs K.M. Rayson
356	Stewart Thornhill	419	Jill & Bill Quibell
357	S.R. Lee	420	G.D. Reeve
358	Patrick Preston	421	
359	June B. Reed	422	O.M. Harper
360	Joan M. Peach	423	M.E. Hilton
361	Sue & Stuart Roderick	424	John Whiting
362	Robert Langford	425	Roy Barrett
363	G.E. Taylor	426	D.L. Carrington
364	Mr & Mrs J.E. Palmer	427	Dr & Mrs D.E. White
365	Brian Haynes	428	J. Pearman
366	T. James Hazelden	429	Gwen Pepper
367	Mrs A.V. Clapton	430	Sarah Wheatley
368	R.N. Claricoats	431	R. Illingsworth
369	F.D. Sewell	432	Chris Farmer
370	C. Coddington	433	D.L.T. Edwards
371	Peter Rollings	434	John Whitehead
372	Yolande Coleman	435	T. Box
373	Rev James T. Farley	436	Ian Norris
374	J.R. Hazelden	437	C.D. Bend
375	C. Spensley	438	Mr & Mrs T. Lamb
376	Ian Kitchener	439	Mrs C.L. Hughes
377	Mr & Mrs A. Woodhouse	440	Raymond Simmons
378	David J. Coot	441	I. Robinson
379	T.E. Keen	442	Mrs E. Figgitt
380	George Norris	443	G.R. & M.L. Nevitte
		444	Anne Ellis
		445	R.E. Baker
		446	E.P. Evans
		447	John Simpson
		448	H.C. Turner
		449	J.E. Harris
		450	Mrs A. Todd

148

Remaining names unlisted

RECTORY FARM

LOT 382

308

307

Allotment
Gardens

THE NOOK

P̲I̲N̲F̲O̲L̲D̲ L̲A̲N̲E̲

LOT 358

304

PT 306

LOT 393

PT 306

LOT 428

LOT 394

THE CHESTNUTS

LOT
389

LOT 391

Meth Chapel

LOT 390

THE FERNS

H̲I̲G̲H̲

LOT 396 LOT

LOT 392

ALBERT ST

S̲T̲

P.O

Allotment
Gardens

oW

Note.—This Plan is based upon the
Ordnance Survey Map with the
sanction of the Controller of H.M.
Stationery Office.